HBR'S 10 MUST READS

On
Strengthening
Your Soft Skills

HBR's 10 Must Reads series is the definitive collection of ideas and best practices for aspiring and experienced leaders alike. These books offer essential reading selected from the pages of *Harvard Business Review* on topics critical to the success of every manager.

Titles include:

HBR's 10 Must Reads 2015
HBR's 10 Must Reads 2016
HBR's 10 Must Reads 2017
HBR's 10 Must Reads 2018
HBR's 10 Must Reads 2019
HBR's 10 Must Reads 2020
HBR's 10 Must Reads 2021
HBR's 10 Must Reads 2022
HBR's 10 Must Reads 2023
HBR's 10 Must Reads 2024
HBR's 10 Must Reads for Business Students
HBR's 10 Must Reads for CEOs
HBR's 10 Must Reads for Executive Teams
HBR's 10 Must Reads for Mid-Level Managers
HBR's 10 Must Reads for New Managers
HBR's 10 Must Reads on AI
HBR's 10 Must Reads on AI, Analytics, and the New Machine Age
HBR's 10 Must Reads on Boards
HBR's 10 Must Reads on Building a Great Culture
HBR's 10 Must Reads on Business Model Innovation
HBR's 10 Must Reads on Career Resilience
HBR's 10 Must Reads on Change Management (Volumes 1 and 2)
HBR's 10 Must Reads on Collaboration
HBR's 10 Must Reads on Communication (Volumes 1 and 2)
HBR's 10 Must Reads on Creativity
HBR's 10 Must Reads on Design Thinking
HBR's 10 Must Reads on Diversity

HBR'S 10 MUST READS

On
Strengthening
Your Soft
Skills

HARVARD BUSINESS REVIEW PRESS
Boston, Massachusetts

HBR Press Quantity Sales Discounts

Harvard Business Review Press titles are available at significant quantity discounts when purchased in bulk for client gifts, sales promotions, and premiums. Special editions, including books with corporate logos, customized covers, and letters from the company or CEO printed in the front matter, as well as excerpts of existing books, can also be created in large quantities for special needs.

For details and discount information for both print and ebook formats, contact booksales@harvardbusiness.org, tel. 800-988-0886, or www.hbr.org/bulksales.

Copyright 2024 Harvard Business School Publishing Corporation

The web addresses referenced in this book were live and correct at the time of the book's publication but may be subject to change.

Cataloging-in-Publication data is forthcoming.

Library of Congress Cataloging-in-Publication Data

Names: Harvard Business Review Press, author.
Title: HBR's 10 must reads on strengthening your soft skills / Harvard
    Business Review.
Description: Boston, Massachusetts : Harvard Business Review Press, [2023] |
    Series: HBR's 10 must reads | Includes index. | Provided by publisher.
Identifiers: LCCN 2023046545 (print) | LCCN 2023046546 (ebook) |
    ISBN 9781647826963 (paperback) | ISBN 9781647826970 (epub)
Subjects: LCSH: Success in business. | Soft skills. | Leadership.
Classification: LCC HF5386 .H2765 2023 (print) | LCC HF5386 (ebook) |
    DDC 650.1—dc23/eng/20231128
LC record available at https://lccn.loc.gov/2023046545
LC ebook record available at https://lccn.loc.gov/2023046546

ISBN: 978-1-64782-696-3
eISBN: 978-1-64782-697-0

Contents

On
Strengthening
Your Soft Skills

The C-Suite Skills
That Matter Most

by Raffaella Sadun, Joseph Fuller, Stephen Hansen, and PJ Neal

FOR A LONG TIME, whenever companies wanted to hire a CEO or another key executive, they knew what to look for: somebody with technical expertise, superior administrative skills, and a track record of successfully managing financial resources. When courting outside candidates to fill those roles, they often favored executives from companies such as GE, IBM, and P&G and from professional-services giants such as McKinsey and Deloitte, which had a reputation for cultivating those skills in their managers.

That practice now feels like ancient history. So much has changed during the past two decades that companies can no longer assume that leaders with traditional managerial pedigrees will succeed in the C-suite. Today firms need to hire executives who are able to motivate diverse, technologically savvy, and global workforces; who can play the role of corporate statesperson, dealing effectively with constituents ranging from sovereign governments to influential NGOs; and who can rapidly and effectively apply their skills in a new company, in what may be an unfamiliar industry, and often with colleagues in the C-suite whom they didn't previously know.

These changes present a phenomenal challenge for executive recruitment, because the capabilities required of top leaders include new and often "softer" skills that are rarely explicitly recognized or fostered in the corporate world. Simply put, it's getting harder and less prudent to rely on traditional indicators of managerial potential.

What should organizations do to face this challenge? A critical first step is to develop greater clarity about what it now takes for C-suite executives to succeed. Yes, the range of necessary skills appears to have expanded—but how exactly? For example, what does the term "soft skills" really mean? And to what extent does the need to hire executives with more-expansive skills vary across organizations?

Remarkably, even though almost every aspect of leadership has been scrutinized in recent years, rigorous evidence on these crucial points is scant. To find out more—about the capabilities that are now in demand, how those have changed over time, and what adjustments companies are making to their process for selecting candidates—we recently analyzed data from Russell Reynolds Associates, one of the world's premier executive-search firms. Russell Reynolds and its competitors play an essential role in managerial labor markets: 80% to 90% of the *Fortune* 250 and FTSE 100 companies use the services of such firms when making a succession decision that involves a choice among candidates. (Disclosure: Russell Reynolds has recently conducted executive searches for Harvard Business Publishing, which publishes *Harvard Business Review*.)

For our research, Russell Reynolds gave us unprecedented access to nearly 5,000 job descriptions that it had developed in collaboration with its clients from 2000 to 2017. The data was sufficient to study expectations not just for the CEO but also for four other key leaders in the C-suite: the chief financial officer, the chief information officer, the head of human resources, and the chief marketing officer. To our knowledge, researchers had never before analyzed such a comprehensive collection of senior-executive job descriptions. (For more about how we worked with the data, see the sidebar "About the Research.")

Our study yielded a variety of insights. Chief among them is this: Over the past two decades, companies have significantly redefined

Idea in Brief

The Shift

It's no longer safe to assume that leaders with traditional managerial pedigrees will succeed in the C-suite. An analysis of executive-search data shows that companies today are prioritizing social skills above technical know-how, expertise in financial stewardship, and other qualifications.

The Explanation

Large companies today have increasingly complex operations, heavier reliance on technology, more workforce diversity, and greater public accountability for their behavior. Leading under those circumstances requires superior listening and communication skills and an ability to relate well to multiple constituencies.

The Path Forward

To succeed in the years ahead, companies will have to figure out how to effectively evaluate the social skills of job candidates. They will also need to make such skills an integral part of their talent-management strategies.

the roles of C-suite executives. The traditional capabilities mentioned earlier—notably the management of financial and operational resources—remain highly relevant. But when companies today search for top leaders, especially new CEOs, they attribute less importance to those capabilities than they used to and instead prioritize one qualification above all others: strong social skills. (See the exhibit "Help wanted: CEOs who are good with people.")

When we refer to "social skills," we mean certain specific capabilities, including a high level of self-awareness, the ability to listen and communicate well, a facility for working with different types of people and groups, and what psychologists call "theory of mind"— the capacity to infer how others are thinking and feeling. The magnitude of the shift in recent years toward these capabilities is most significant for CEOs but also pronounced for the four other C-suite roles we studied.

Our analysis revealed that social skills are particularly important in settings where productivity hinges on effective communication, as it invariably does in the large, complex, and skill-intensive enterprises

About the Research

THIS ARTICLE IS BASED ON a rich data set drawn from almost 5,000 job descriptions compiled by Russell Reynolds Associates and companies conducting searches for various C-suite positions. Translating that data into variables that were amenable to quantitative analysis was no easy feat, because the job descriptions did not follow a standard structure or contain standard content. Our approach involved two steps.

First we defined a distinctive set of skill requirements that were relevant for chief executives. We started by combing through the U.S. Department of Labor's O*NET database (a repository of information about more than 1,000 occupations) to see what skills were listed for "chief executive" roles. We then sorted those into six clusters that included similar tasks: managing financial and material resources; monitoring corporate performance; tending to human resources; handling administrative tasks; processing and using complex information; and exercising social skills.

Our second step was to determine the extent to which each job description provided by Russell Reynolds was semantically similar to each O*NET skills cluster.

Both steps relied on a model of managerial language that we developed by applying cutting-edge machine-learning techniques (word2vec) to a corpus composed of every *Harvard Business Review* article published since the magazine's inception in 1922.

---

that employ executive search firms. In such organizations, CEOs and other senior leaders can't limit themselves to performing routine operational tasks. They also have to spend a significant amount of time interacting with others and enabling coordination—by communicating information, facilitating the exchange of ideas, building and overseeing teams, and identifying and solving problems.

Intriguingly, the evolution of skills requirements in the C-suite parallels developments in the workforce as a whole. At all employment levels today, more and more jobs require highly developed social skills. Harvard's David Deming, among others, has demonstrated that such jobs have grown at a faster rate than the labor market as a whole—and that compensation for them is growing faster than average.

Help wanted: CEOs who are good with people

Since 2007, companies advertising C-suite openings have increasingly emphasized the importance of social skills and de-emphasized operational expertise.

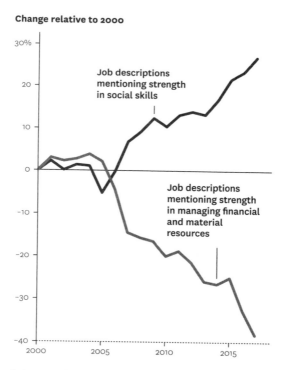

Change relative to 2000

Job descriptions mentioning strength in social skills

Job descriptions mentioning strength in managing financial and material resources

Note: Job descriptions were for nearly 5,000 C-suite positions advertised by the executive-search firm Russell Reynolds Associates. The data points were estimated in a regression model that controls for industry differences and other variables. The coefficients after 2007 are significantly different from zero across both skill clusters.

Why is this shift toward social skills taking place? And what implications does it have for executive development, CEO succession planning, and the organization of the C-suite? This article offers some preliminary thoughts.

The Chief Reasons for Change

We've identified two main drivers of the growing demand for social skills.

Firm size and complexity

The focus on social skills is especially evident in large firms. Additionally, among firms of similar size, the demand for social skills is greater at publicly listed multinational enterprises and those that are involved in mergers and acquisitions. These patterns are consistent with the view that in larger and more complex organizations, top managers are increasingly expected to coordinate disparate and specialized knowledge, match the organization's problems with people who can solve them, and effectively orchestrate internal communication. For all those tasks, it helps to be able to interact well with others.

But the importance of social skills in large companies arises from more than just the complexity of operations there. It also reflects the web of critical relationships that leaders at such firms must cultivate and maintain with outside constituencies.

The diversity and number of those relationships can be daunting. Executives at public companies have to worry not only about product markets but also about capital markets. They need to brief analysts, woo asset managers, and address the business press. They must respond to various kinds of regulators across multiple jurisdictions. They're expected to communicate well with key customers and suppliers. During mergers and acquisitions, they have to attend carefully to constituents who are important to closing the transaction and supporting the post-merger integration. Highly developed social skills are critical to success in all those arenas.

Information-processing technologies

"The more we automate information handling," management guru Peter Drucker wrote several decades ago, "the more we will have to create opportunities for effective communication." That has turned out to be prescient: Companies that rely significantly on information-processing technologies today also tend to be those that need leaders with especially strong social skills.

Here's why. Increasingly, in every part of the organization, when companies automate routine tasks, their competitiveness hinges on capabilities that computer systems simply don't have—things such as judgment, creativity, and perception. In technologically intensive firms, where automation is widespread, leaders have to align a heterogeneous workforce, respond to unexpected events, and manage conflict in the decision-making process, all of which are best done by managers with strong social skills.

Moreover, most companies today rely on many of the same technological platforms—Amazon Web Services, Facebook, Google, Microsoft, Salesforce, Workday. That means they have less opportunity to differentiate themselves on the basis of tangible technological investments alone. When every major competitor in a market leverages the same suite of tools, leaders need to distinguish themselves through superior management of the people who use those tools. That requires them to be top-notch communicators in every regard, able both to devise the right messages and to deliver them with empathy.

In sum, as more tasks are entrusted to technology, workers with superior social skills will be in demand at all levels and will command a premium in the labor market.

Other Factors

Our research suggests that the growing interest in social skills is being spurred by two additional drivers. These are harder to quantify, but they nonetheless may play an important role in the shift that's taking place.

Social media and networking technologies

Historically, CEOs didn't attract much popular notice, nor did they seek the limelight. While other businesspeople, investors, and members of the business press paid attention to them, the public generally did not, except in the cases of "celebrity" CEOs such as GE's Jack Welch, Sony's Akio Morita, and Chrysler's Lee Iacocca.

That era is over. As companies move away from shareholder primacy and focus more broadly on stakeholder capitalism, CEOs and other senior leaders are expected to be public figures. They're obliged not only to interact with an increasingly broad range of internal and external constituencies but to do so personally and transparently and accountably. No longer can they rely on support functions—the corporate communications team, the government relations department, and so forth—to take care of all those relationships.

Furthermore, top leaders must manage interactions in real time, thanks to the increasing prevalence of both social media (which can capture and publicize missteps nearly instantaneously) and network platforms such as Slack and Glassdoor (which allow employees to widely disseminate information and opinions about their colleagues and bosses).

In the past, too, executives were expected to be able to explain and defend everything from their business strategies to their HR practices. But they did so in a controlled environment, at a time and a place of management's choosing. Now they must be constantly attuned to how their decisions are perceived by various audiences. Failing to achieve their intended purposes with even a handful of employees or other constituents can be damaging.

So social skills matter greatly. The occupants of the C-suite need to be adroit at communicating spontaneously and anticipating how their words and actions will play beyond the immediate context.

Diversity and inclusion

Another new challenge for CEOs and other senior leaders is dealing with issues of diversity and inclusion—publicly, empathetically, and proactively. That, too, demands strong social skills, particularly theory of mind. Executives who possess that perceptiveness about the mental states of others can move more easily among various employee groups, make them feel heard, and represent their interests within the organization, to the board of directors, and to outside constituencies. More importantly, they can nurture an environment in which diverse talent thrives.

New Areas for Focus

Given the critical role that social skills play in leadership success today, companies will need to refocus on the following areas as they hire and cultivate new leaders.

Systematically building social skills

Traditionally, boards and senior executives have cultivated future leaders by rotating them through critical departments and functions, posting them to various geographic locations, and putting them through executive development programs. It was assumed that the best way to prepare promising managers for a future in the C-suite was to have them develop deep competence in a variety of administrative and operational roles.

With this model, evaluating success and failure was reasonably straightforward. Processes ran smoothly or they didn't; results were achieved or they weren't. Social skills mattered, of course: As up-and-comers moved through functions and geographies, their ability to quickly form constructive relationships with colleagues, customers, regulators, and suppliers affected their performance. But such skills were considered something of a bonus. They were a means to achieving operational objectives (a prerequisite for advancement) and were seldom evaluated in an explicit, systematic, and objective way.

Companies today better appreciate the importance of social skills in executive performance, but they've made little progress in devising processes for evaluating a candidate's proficiency in those skills and determining aptitude for further growth. Few companies invest in training to improve the interviewing skills of staffers involved in recruiting—least of all senior executives or independent directors, who are presumed to have the background and perspective necessary to make sound judgments.

Getting references is also problematic: Companies typically conduct senior-level searches with a high degree of confidentiality, both to protect themselves (a leak could cost them the best prospect) and to protect the candidates (who might not want their employers to know that they're open to job offers). Moreover, the people conducting C-suite interviews and those providing references are likely to be part of the same small, homogeneous networks as most of the candidates, which significantly heightens the risk of bias in the decision-making process. For example, board members tend to support candidates who are referred by friends or have backgrounds similar to their own. They might mistakenly assume that those individuals possess broadly applicable social skills simply because they connected easily with them in interviews.

To better evaluate social skills, some companies now run psychometric assessments or simulations. Psychometric tests (which are designed to measure personality traits and behavioral style) can help establish whether someone is outgoing and comfortable with strangers, but they shed little light on how effective that person will be when interacting with various groups. Simulation exercises, for their part, have been used for some time to evaluate how individuals respond to challenging circumstances, but they're usually designed around a specific scenario, such as a product-integrity crisis or the arrival of an activist investor on the scene. Simulations are best at assessing candidates' administrative and technical skills in such situations, rather than their ability to coordinate teams or interact spontaneously with diverse constituencies. Even so, these exercises are not widely used, because of the time and money required to run them well.

In their executive development programs, companies today need a systematic approach to building and evaluating social skills. They may even need to prioritize them over the "hard" skills that managers presently favor because they're so easy to assess. Companies should place high-potential leaders in positions that oblige them to interact with various employee populations and external constituencies and then closely monitor their performance in those roles.

Assessing social skills innovatively

The criteria that companies have traditionally used to size up candidates for C-suite positions—such as work history, technical qualifications, and career trajectory—are of limited value in assessing social skills. Companies will need to create new tools if they are to establish an objective basis for evaluating and comparing people's abilities in this realm. They can act either independently or in conjunction with the professional-services firms that support them, but in either case they'll need to custom-design solutions to serve their particular needs.

Although appropriate tools have yet to be developed for searches at the highest echelons of organizations, considerable innovation is underway when it comes to ascertaining the skills of lower-level job seekers and placing them in the right positions. Companies such as Eightfold and Gloat, for example, are using artificial intelligence to improve matching between candidates and employers. New custom tools are also being used to identify skill adjacencies and to create internal talent marketplaces, helping companies assign qualified employees to important tasks more quickly. The underlying algorithms rely on huge data sets, which poses a technological challenge, but this approach holds promise for executive recruiting.

Similarly, pymetrics, among other companies, is mining world-class behavioral research to see how particular candidates fit with an organization or a specific position. Such an approach has proved useful in evaluating a broad array of soft skills and in reducing bias in recruiting. Recent academic work shows the utility of tapping into behavioral research: Harvard's Ben Weidmann and David Deming, for example, have found that the Reading the Mind in the Eyes Test, a well-established measure of social intelligence, can effectively predict the performance of individuals in team settings. If companies develop new tests based on the same design principles, they and their boards of directors should be able to gain a fuller and more objective understanding of the social skills of C-suite candidates.

Emphasizing social skills development at all levels

Companies that rely on outside hiring to find executives with superior social skills are playing a dangerous game. For one thing, competition for such people will become fierce. For another, it's inherently risky to put an outsider—even someone carefully vetted—in a senior role. Companies thus will benefit from a "grow your own" approach that allows internal up-and-comers to hone and demonstrate a range of interpersonal abilities.

Assessing the collective social skills in the C-suite

Increasingly, boards of directors and company executives will need to develop and evaluate the social skills of not only individual leaders but the C-suite as a whole. Weakness or ineptitude on the part of any one person on the team will have a systems effect on the group—and especially the CEO. Companies recognize this: Social skills are gaining in relative importance in the search criteria for all five of the executive positions we studied. Moreover, as CEOs continue playing a bigger role in constituency and personnel management, the responsibilities within the C-suite may be reconfigured, and other executives will need strong social skills too.

The Way Forward

As we've established, companies still value C-suite executives with traditional administrative and operational skills. But they're increasingly on the lookout for people with highly developed social skills—especially if their organizations are large, complex, and technologically intensive.

Will companies, however, actually succeed in making different kinds of hires? That's an open question. The answer will depend in part on whether they can figure out how to effectively evaluate the social skills of job candidates, and whether they decide to make the cultivation of social skills an integral component of their talent-management strategies.

In our view, companies are going to have to do both those things to remain competitive. To that end, they should encourage business schools and other educators to place more emphasis on social skills in their MBA and executive-level curricula, and they should challenge search firms and other intermediaries to devise innovative mechanisms for identifying and assessing candidates.

Companies themselves will also have to do things differently. In recruiting and evaluating outside talent, they must prioritize social skills. The same is true when it comes to measuring the performance of current executives and setting their compensation. In addition, firms should make strong social skills a criterion for promotion, and they should task supervisors with nurturing such skills in high-potential subordinates.

In the years ahead, some companies may focus on trying to better identify and hire leaders with "the right stuff"; others may pay more attention to executive training and retention. But no matter what approach they adopt, it's clear that to succeed in an increasingly challenging business environment, they'll have to profoundly rethink their current practices.

Originally published in July–August 2022. Reprint S22041

The Focused Leader

by Daniel Goleman

A PRIMARY TASK OF LEADERSHIP is to direct attention. To do so, leaders must learn to focus their own attention. When we speak about being focused, we commonly mean thinking about one thing while filtering out distractions. But a wealth of recent research in neuroscience shows that we focus in many ways, for different purposes, drawing on different neural pathways—some of which work in concert, while others tend to stand in opposition.

Grouping these modes of attention into three broad buckets— focusing on *yourself,* focusing on *others,* and focusing on *the wider world*—sheds new light on the practice of many essential leadership skills. Focusing inward and focusing constructively on others helps leaders cultivate the primary elements of emotional intelligence. A fuller understanding of how they focus on the wider world can improve their ability to devise strategy, innovate, and manage organizations.

Every leader needs to cultivate this triad of awareness, in abundance and in the proper balance, because a failure to focus inward leaves you rudderless, a failure to focus on others renders you clueless, and a failure to focus outward may leave you blindsided.

Focusing on Yourself

Emotional intelligence begins with self-awareness—getting in touch with your inner voice. Leaders who heed their inner voices can draw on more resources to make better decisions and connect with their authentic selves. But what does that entail? A look at how people focus inward can make this abstract concept more concrete.

Self-awareness

Hearing your inner voice is a matter of paying careful attention to internal physiological signals. These subtle cues are monitored by the insula, which is tucked behind the frontal lobes of the brain. Attention given to any part of the body amps up the insula's sensitivity to that part. Tune in to your heartbeat, and the insula activates more neurons in that circuitry. How well people can sense their heartbeats has, in fact, become a standard way to measure their self-awareness.

Gut feelings are messages from the insula and the amygdala, which the neuroscientist Antonio Damasio, of the University of Southern California, calls *somatic markers*. Those messages are sensations that something "feels" right or wrong. Somatic markers simplify decision making by guiding our attention toward better options. They're hardly foolproof (how often was that feeling that you left the stove on correct?), so the more comprehensively we read them, the better we use our intuition. (See "Are You Skimming This Sidebar?")

Consider, for example, the implications of an analysis of interviews conducted by a group of British researchers with 118 professional traders and 10 senior managers at four City of London investment banks. The most successful traders (whose annual income averaged £500,000) were neither the ones who relied entirely on analytics nor the ones who just went with their guts. They focused on a full range of emotions, which they used to judge the value of their intuition. When they suffered losses, they acknowledged their anxiety, became more cautious, and took fewer risks. The least successful traders (whose income averaged only £100,000) tended to ignore their anxiety and keep going with their guts. Because they failed to heed a wider array of internal signals, they were misled.

Zeroing in on sensory impressions of ourselves in the moment is one major element of self-awareness. But another is critical to leadership: combining our experiences across time into a coherent view of our authentic selves.

Idea in Brief

The Problem

A primary task of leadership is to direct attention. To do so, leaders must learn to focus their own attention.

The Argument

People commonly think of "being focused" as filtering out distractions while concentrating on one thing. But a wealth of recent neuroscience research shows that we focus attention in many ways, for different purposes, while drawing on different neural pathways.

The Solution

Every leader needs to cultivate a triad of awareness—an inward focus, a focus on others, and an outward focus. Focusing inward and focusing on others helps leaders cultivate emotional intelligence. Focusing outward can improve their ability to devise strategy, innovate, and manage organizations.

To be authentic is to be the same person to others as you are to yourself. In part that entails paying attention to what others think of you, particularly people whose opinions you esteem and who will be candid in their feedback. A variety of focus that is useful here is *open awareness,* in which we broadly notice what's going on around us without getting caught up in or swept away by any particular thing. In this mode we don't judge, censor, or tune out; we simply perceive.

Leaders who are more accustomed to giving input than to receiving it may find this tricky. Someone who has trouble sustaining open awareness typically gets snagged by irritating details, such as fellow travelers in the airport security line who take forever getting their carry-ons into the scanner. Someone who can keep her attention in open mode will notice the travelers but not worry about them, and will take in more of her surroundings. (See the sidebar "Expand Your Awareness.")

Of course, being open to input doesn't guarantee that someone will provide it. Sadly, life affords us few chances to learn how others really see us, and even fewer for executives as they rise through the ranks. That may be why one of the most popular and overenrolled courses at Harvard Business School is Bill George's Authentic Leadership Development, in which George has created what he calls True North groups to heighten this aspect of self-awareness.

Are You Skimming This Sidebar?

DO YOU HAVE TROUBLE remembering what someone has just told you in conversation? Did you drive to work this morning on autopilot? Do you focus more on your smartphone than on the person you're having lunch with?

Attention is a mental muscle; like any other muscle, it can be strengthened through the right kind of exercise. The fundamental rep for building deliberate attention is simple: When your mind wanders, notice that it has wandered, bring it back to your desired point of focus, and keep it there as long as you can. That basic exercise is at the root of virtually every kind of meditation. Meditation builds concentration and calmness and facilitates recovery from the agitation of stress.

So does a video game called Tenacity, now in development by a design group and neuroscientists at the University of Wisconsin. Slated for release in 2014, the game offers a leisurely journey through any of half a dozen scenes, from a barren desert to a fantasy staircase spiraling heavenward. At the beginner's level you tap an iPad screen with one finger every time you exhale; the challenge is to tap two fingers with every fifth breath. As you move to higher levels, you're presented with more distractions—a helicopter flies into view, a plane does a flip, a flock of birds suddenly scud by.

When players are attuned to the rhythm of their breathing, they experience the strengthening of selective attention as a feeling of calm focus, as in meditation. Stanford University is exploring that connection at its Calming Technology Lab, which is developing relaxing devices, such as a belt that detects your breathing rate. Should a chock-full inbox, for instance, trigger what has been called email apnea, an iPhone app can guide you through exercises to calm your breathing and your mind.

These groups (which anyone can form) are based on the precept that self-knowledge begins with self-revelation. Accordingly, they are open and intimate, "a safe place," George explains, "where members can discuss personal issues they do not feel they can raise elsewhere—often not even with their closest family members." What good does that do? "We don't know who we are until we hear ourselves speaking the story of our lives to those we trust," George says. It's a structured way to match our view of our true selves with the views our most trusted colleagues have—an external check on our authenticity.

Expand Your Awareness

JUST AS A CAMERA LENS can be set narrowly on a single point or more widely to take in a panoramic view, you can focus tightly or expansively.

One measure of open awareness presents people with a stream of letters and numbers, such as S, K, O, E, 4, R, T, 2, H, P. In scanning the stream, many people will notice the first number, 4, but after that their attention blinks. Those firmly in open awareness mode will register the second number as well.

Strengthening the ability to maintain open awareness requires leaders to do something that verges on the unnatural: cultivate at least sometimes a willingness to not be in control, not offer up their own views, not judge others. That's less a matter of deliberate action than of attitude adjustment.

One path to making that adjustment is through the classic power of positive thinking, because pessimism narrows our focus, whereas positive emotions widen our attention and our receptiveness to the new and unexpected. A simple way to shift into positive mode is to ask yourself, "If everything worked out perfectly in my life, what would I be doing in 10 years?" Why is that effective? Because when you're in an upbeat mood, the University of Wisconsin neuroscientist Richard Davidson has found, your brain's left prefrontal area lights up. That area harbors the circuitry that reminds us how great we'll feel when we reach some long-sought goal.

"Talking about positive goals and dreams activates brain centers that open you up to new possibilities," says Richard Boyatzis, a psychologist at Case Western Reserve. "But if you change the conversation to what you should do to fix yourself, it closes you down. . . . You need the negative to survive, but the positive to thrive."

Self-control

"Cognitive control" is the scientific term for putting one's attention where one wants it and keeping it there in the face of temptation to wander. This focus is one aspect of the brain's executive function, which is located in the prefrontal cortex. A colloquial term for it is "willpower."

Cognitive control enables executives to pursue a goal despite distractions and setbacks. The same neural circuitry that allows such a single-minded pursuit of goals also manages unruly emotions. Good cognitive control can be seen in people who stay calm in a crisis, tame their own agitation, and recover from a debacle or defeat.

Decades' worth of research demonstrates the singular importance of willpower to leadership success. Particularly compelling is a longitudinal study tracking the fates of all 1,037 children born during a single year in the 1970s in the New Zealand city of Dunedin. For several years during childhood the children were given a battery of tests of willpower, including the psychologist Walter Mischel's legendary "marshmallow test"—a choice between eating one marshmallow right away and getting two by waiting 15 minutes. In Mischel's experiments, roughly a third of children grab the marshmallow on the spot, another third hold out for a while longer, and a third manage to make it through the entire quarter hour.

Years later, when the children in the Dunedin study were in their 30s and all but 4% of them had been tracked down again, the researchers found that those who'd had the cognitive control to resist the marshmallow longest were significantly healthier, more successful financially, and more law-abiding than the ones who'd been unable to hold out at all. In fact, statistical analysis showed that a child's level of self-control was a more powerful predictor of financial success than IQ, social class, or family circumstance.

How we focus holds the key to exercising willpower, Mischel says. Three subvarieties of cognitive control are at play when you pit self-restraint against self-gratification: the ability to voluntarily disengage your focus from an object of desire; the ability to resist distraction so that you don't gravitate back to that object; and the ability to concentrate on the future goal and imagine how good you will feel when you achieve it. As adults the children of Dunedin may have been held hostage to their younger selves, but they need not have been, because the power to focus can be developed. (See the sidebar "Learning Self-Restraint.")

Focusing on Others

The word "attention" comes from the Latin *attendere*, meaning "to reach toward." This is a perfect definition of focus on others, which is the foundation of empathy and of an ability to build social relationships—the second and third pillars of emotional intelligence.

Learning Self-Restraint

QUICK, NOW. HERE'S A TEST of cognitive control. In what direction is the middle arrow in each row pointing?

→ → → ← ←
→ ← ← ← ←
→ → ← → →

The test, called the Eriksen Flanker Task, gauges your susceptibility to distraction. When it's taken under laboratory conditions, differences of a thousandth of a second can be detected in the speed with which subjects perceive which direction the middle arrows are pointing. The stronger their cognitive control, the less susceptible they are to distraction.

Interventions to strengthen cognitive control can be as unsophisticated as a game of Simon Says or Red Light—any exercise in which you are asked to stop on cue. Research suggests that the better a child gets at playing Musical Chairs, the stronger their prefrontal wiring for cognitive control will become.

Operating on a similarly simple principle is a social and emotional learning (SEL) method that's used to strengthen cognitive control in schoolchildren across the United States. When confronted by an upsetting problem, the children are told to think of a traffic signal. The red light means stop, calm down, and think before you act. The yellow light means slow down and think of several possible solutions. The green light means try out a plan and see how it works. Thinking in these terms allows the children to shift away from amygdala-driven impulses to prefrontal-driven deliberate behavior.

It's never too late for adults to strengthen these circuits as well. Daily sessions of mindfulness practice work in a way similar to Musical Chairs and SEL. In these sessions you focus your attention on your breathing and practice tracking your thoughts and feelings without getting swept away by them. Whenever you notice that your mind has wandered, you simply return it to your breath. It sounds easy—but try it for 10 minutes, and you'll find there's a learning curve.

Executives who can effectively focus on others are easy to recognize. They are the ones who find common ground, whose opinions carry the most weight, and with whom other people want to work. They emerge as natural leaders regardless of organizational or social rank.

The empathy triad

We talk about empathy most commonly as a single attribute. But a close look at where leaders are focusing when they exhibit it reveals three distinct kinds, each important for leadership effectiveness:

- *cognitive empathy*—the ability to understand another person's perspective;

- *emotional empathy*—the ability to feel what someone else feels;

- *empathic concern*—the ability to sense what another person needs from you.

Cognitive empathy enables leaders to explain themselves in meaningful ways—a skill essential to getting the best performance from their direct reports. Contrary to what you might expect, exercising cognitive empathy requires leaders to think about feelings rather than to feel them directly.

An inquisitive nature feeds cognitive empathy. As one successful executive with this trait puts it, "I've always just wanted to learn everything, to understand anybody that I was around—why they thought what they did, why they did what they did, what worked for them, and what didn't work." But cognitive empathy is also an outgrowth of self-awareness. The executive circuits that allow us to think about our own thoughts and to monitor the feelings that flow from them let us apply the same reasoning to other people's minds when we choose to direct our attention that way.

Emotional empathy is important for effective mentoring, managing clients, and reading group dynamics. It springs from ancient parts of the brain beneath the cortex—the amygdala, the hypothalamus, the hippocampus, and the orbitofrontal cortex—that allow us to feel fast without thinking deeply. They tune us in by arousing in our bodies the emotional states of others: I literally feel your pain. My brain patterns match up with yours when I listen to you tell a gripping story. As Tania Singer, the director of the social neuroscience department at the Max Planck Institute for Human Cognitive and Brain Sciences, in Leipzig, says, "You need to understand your own feelings to understand the feelings of others." Accessing your capacity for emotional empathy depends on combining two kinds of attention: a deliberate focus on your own echoes of someone else's

When Empathy Needs to Be Learned

EMOTIONAL EMPATHY CAN BE DEVELOPED. That's the conclusion suggested by research conducted with physicians by Helen Riess, the director of the Empathy and Relational Science Program at Boston's Massachusetts General Hospital. To help the physicians monitor themselves, she set up a program in which they learned to focus using deep, diaphragmatic breathing and to cultivate a certain detachment—to watch an interaction from the ceiling, as it were, rather than being lost in their own thoughts and feelings. "Suspending your own involvement to observe what's going on gives you a mindful awareness of the interaction without being completely reactive," says Riess. "You can see if your own physiology is charged up or balanced. You can notice what's transpiring in the situation." If a doctor realizes that she's feeling irritated, for instance, that may be a signal that the patient is bothered too.

Those who are utterly at a loss may be able to prime emotional empathy essentially by faking it until they make it, Riess adds. If you act in a caring way—looking people in the eye and paying attention to their expressions, even when you don't particularly want to—you may start to feel more engaged.

feelings and an open awareness of that person's face, voice, and other external signs of emotion. (See the sidebar "When Empathy Needs to Be Learned.")

Empathic concern, which is closely related to emotional empathy, enables you to sense not just how people feel but what they need from you. It's what you want in your doctor, your spouse—and your boss. Empathic concern has its roots in the circuitry that compels parents' attention to their children. Watch where people's eyes go when someone brings an adorable baby into a room, and you'll see this mammalian brain center leaping into action.

One neural theory holds that the response is triggered in the amygdala by the brain's radar for sensing danger and in the prefrontal cortex by the release of oxytocin, the chemical for caring. This implies that empathic concern is a double-edged feeling. We intuitively experience the distress of another as our own. But in deciding whether we will meet that person's needs, we deliberately weigh how much we value their well-being.

Getting this intuition-deliberation mix right has great implications. Those whose sympathetic feelings become too strong may themselves suffer. In the helping professions, this can lead to

When Empathy Needs to Be Controlled

GETTING A GRIP on our impulse to empathize with other people's feelings can help us make better decisions when someone's emotional flood threatens to overwhelm us.

Ordinarily, when we see someone pricked with a pin, our brains emit a signal indicating that our own pain centers are echoing that distress. But physicians learn in medical school to block even such automatic responses. Their attentional anesthetic seems to be deployed by the temporal-parietal junction and regions of the prefrontal cortex, a circuit that boosts concentration by tuning out emotions. That's what is happening in your brain when you distance yourself from others in order to stay calm and help them. The same neural network kicks in when we see a problem in an emotionally overheated environment and need to focus on looking for a solution. If you're talking with someone who is upset, this system helps you understand the person's perspective intellectually by shifting from the heart-to-heart of emotional empathy to the head-to-heart of cognitive empathy.

---

compassion fatigue; in executives, it can create distracting feelings of anxiety about people and circumstances that are beyond anyone's control. But those who protect themselves by deadening their feelings may lose touch with empathy. Empathic concern requires us to manage our personal distress without numbing ourselves to the pain of others. (See the sidebar "When Empathy Needs to Be Controlled.")

What's more, some lab research suggests that the appropriate application of empathic concern is critical to making moral judgments. Brain scans have revealed that when volunteers listened to tales of people subjected to physical pain, their own brain centers for experiencing such pain lit up instantly. But if the story was about psychological suffering, the higher brain centers involved in empathic concern and compassion took longer to activate. Some time is needed to grasp the psychological and moral dimensions of a situation. The more distracted we are, the less we can cultivate the subtler forms of empathy and compassion.

Building relationships
People who lack social sensitivity are easy to spot—at least for other people. They are the clueless among us. The CFO who is technically

competent but bullies some people, freezes out others, and plays favorites—but when you point out what he has just done, shifts the blame, gets angry, or thinks that you're the problem—is not trying to be a jerk; he's utterly unaware of his shortcomings.

Social sensitivity appears to be related to cognitive empathy. Cognitively empathic executives do better at overseas assignments, for instance, presumably because they quickly pick up implicit norms and learn the unique mental models of a new culture. Attention to social context lets us act with skill no matter what the situation, instinctively follow the universal algorithm for etiquette, and behave in ways that put others at ease. (In another age this might have been called good manners.)

Circuitry that converges on the anterior hippocampus reads social context and leads us intuitively to act differently with, say, our college buddies than with our families or our colleagues. In concert with the deliberative prefrontal cortex, it squelches the impulse to do something inappropriate. Accordingly, one brain test for sensitivity to context assesses the function of the hippocampus. The University of Wisconsin neuroscientist Richard Davidson hypothesizes that people who are most alert to social situations exhibit stronger activity and more connections between the hippocampus and the prefrontal cortex than those who just can't seem to get it right.

The same circuits may be at play when we map social networks in a group—a skill that lets us navigate the relationships in those networks well. People who excel at organizational influence can not only sense the flow of personal connections but also name the people whose opinions hold most sway, and so focus on persuading those who will persuade others.

Alarmingly, research suggests that as people rise through the ranks and gain power, their ability to perceive and maintain personal connections tends to suffer a sort of psychic attrition. In studying encounters between people of varying status, Dacher Keltner, a psychologist at Berkeley, has found that higher-ranking individuals consistently focus their gaze less on lower-ranking people and are more likely to interrupt or to monopolize the conversation.

In fact, mapping attention to power in an organization gives a clear indication of hierarchy: The longer it takes Person A to respond to Person B, the more relative power Person A has. Map response times across an entire organization, and you'll get a remarkably accurate chart of social standing. The boss leaves emails unanswered for hours; those lower down respond within minutes. This is so predictable that an algorithm for it—called automated social hierarchy detection—has been developed at Columbia University. Intelligence agencies reportedly are applying the algorithm to suspected terrorist gangs to piece together chains of influence and identify central figures.

But the real point is this: Where we see ourselves on the social ladder sets the default for how much attention we pay. This should be a warning to top executives, who need to respond to fast-moving competitive situations by tapping the full range of ideas and talents within an organization. Without a deliberate shift in attention, their natural inclination may be to ignore smart ideas from the lower ranks.

Focusing on the Wider World

Leaders with a strong outward focus are not only good listeners but also good questioners. They are visionaries who can sense the far-flung consequences of local decisions and imagine how the choices they make today will play out in the future. They are open to the surprising ways in which seemingly unrelated data can inform their central interests. Melinda Gates offered up a cogent example when she remarked on 60 Minutes that her husband was the kind of person who would read an entire book about fertilizer. Charlie Rose asked, Why fertilizer? The connection was obvious to Bill Gates, who is constantly looking for technological advances that can save lives on a massive scale. "A few billion people would have to die if we hadn't come up with fertilizer," he replied.

Focusing on strategy

Any business school course on strategy will give you the two main elements: exploitation of your current advantage and exploration for new ones. Brain scans that were performed on 63 seasoned business decision makers as they pursued or switched between exploitative and exploratory strategies revealed the specific circuits involved. Not surprisingly, exploitation requires concentration on the job at hand, whereas exploration demands open awareness to recognize new possibilities. But exploitation is accompanied by activity in the brain's circuitry for anticipation and reward. In other words, it feels good to coast along in a familiar routine. When we switch to exploration, we have to make a deliberate cognitive effort to disengage from that routine in order to roam widely and pursue fresh paths.

What keeps us from making that effort? Sleep deprivation, drinking, stress, and mental overload all interfere with the executive circuitry used to make the cognitive switch. To sustain the outward focus that leads to innovation, we need some uninterrupted time in which to reflect and refresh our focus.

The wellsprings of innovation

In an era when almost everyone has access to the same information, new value arises from putting ideas together in novel ways and asking smart questions that open up untapped potential. Moments before we have a creative insight, the brain shows a third-of-a-second spike in gamma waves, indicating the synchrony of far-flung brain cells. The more neurons firing in sync, the bigger the spike. Its timing suggests that what's happening is the formation of a new neural network—presumably creating a fresh association.

But it would be making too much of this to see gamma waves as a secret to creativity. A classic model of creativity suggests how the various modes of attention play key roles. First we prepare our minds by gathering a wide variety of pertinent information, and then we alternate between concentrating intently on the problem and letting our minds wander freely. Those activities translate roughly into vigilance, when while immersing ourselves in all kinds of input, we remain alert for anything relevant to the problem at hand; selective attention to the specific creative challenge; and open awareness, in which we allow our minds to associate freely and the solution to emerge spontaneously. (That's why so many fresh ideas come to people in the shower or out for a walk or a run.)

The dubious gift of systems awareness

If people are given a quick view of a photo of lots of dots and asked to guess how many there are, the strong systems thinkers in the group tend to make the best estimates. This skill shows up in those who are good at designing software, assembly lines, matrix organizations, or interventions to save failing ecosystems—it's a very powerful gift indeed. After all, we live within extremely complex systems. But, suggests the Cambridge University psychologist Simon Baron-Cohen (a cousin of Sacha's), in a small but significant number of people, a strong systems awareness is coupled with an empathy deficit—a blind spot for what other people are thinking and feeling and for reading social situations. For that reason, although people with a superior systems understanding are organizational assets, they are not necessarily effective leaders.

An executive at one bank explained to me that it has created a separate career ladder for systems analysts so that they can progress in status and salary on the basis of their systems smarts alone. That way, the bank can consult them as needed while recruiting leaders from a different pool—one containing people with emotional intelligence.

Putting It All Together

For those who don't want to end up similarly compartmentalized, the message is clear. A focused leader is not the person concentrating on the three most important priorities of the year, or the most brilliant systems thinker, or the one most in tune with the corporate culture. Focused leaders can command the full range of their own attention: They are in touch with their inner feelings, they can control their impulses, they are aware of how others see them, they understand what others need from them, they can weed out distractions and also allow their minds to roam widely, free of preconceptions.

This is challenging. But if great leadership were a paint-by-numbers exercise, great leaders would be more common. Practically every form of focus can be strengthened. What it takes is not talent so much as diligence—a willingness to exercise the attention circuits of the brain just as we exercise our analytic skills and other systems of the body.

The link between attention and excellence remains hidden most of the time. Yet attention is the basis of the most essential of leadership skills—emotional, organizational, and strategic intelligence. And never has it been under greater assault. The constant onslaught of incoming data leads to sloppy shortcuts—triaging our email by reading only the subject lines, skipping many of our voicemails, skimming memos and reports. Not only do our habits of attention make us less effective, but the sheer volume of all those messages leaves us too little time to reflect on what they really mean. This was foreseen more than 40 years ago by the Nobel Prize–winning economist Herbert Simon. Information "consumes the attention of its recipients," he wrote in 1971. "Hence a wealth of information creates a poverty of attention."

My goal here is to place attention center stage so that you can direct it where you need it when you need it. Learn to master your attention, and you will be in command of where you, and your organization, focus.

Originally published in December 2013. Reprint R1312B

Making Empathy Central to Your Company Culture

by Jamil Zaki

IN TIM COOK'S 2017 MIT commencement address, he warned graduates, "People will try to convince you that you should keep empathy out of your career. Don't accept this false premise." The Apple CEO is not alone in recognizing and emphasizing the importance of *empathy*—the ability to share and understand others' emotions—at work. At the time of his remarks, 20% of U.S. employers offered empathy training for managers. In a recent survey of 150 CEOs, over 80% recognized empathy as key to success.[1]

Research demonstrates that Cook and other leaders are onto something. Empathic workplaces tend to enjoy stronger collaboration, less stress, and greater morale, and their employees bounce back more quickly from difficult moments such as layoffs. Still, despite their efforts, many leaders struggle to actually make caring part of their organizational culture. In fact, there's often a gap between the culture executives want and the one they have.

Imagine a company whose culture is defined by aggression and competition. The CEO realizes he and his colleagues can't go on this way, so he hastily rolls out empathy as a key new corporate value. It's a well-intentioned move, but he has shifted the goalposts, creating distance between the organization's *ideals*—prescriptions for how people ought to behave—and its current social *norms*—how most members of a group actually behave. He might hope this will put employees in an aspirational mood, but evidence suggests the opposite. When norms and ideals clash, people gravitate toward *what others do*, not *what they're told* to do. What's worse, people who adhered to the previous culture might feel betrayed or see leadership as hypocritical and out of touch.

Thankfully there's a way to work *with* the power of social norms instead of against them, and consequently change the culture. As I describe in my book, *The War for Kindness*, while people do conform to others' bad behaviors, they also adhere to kind and productive norms. For instance, after seeing others vote, conserve energy, or donate to charity, people are more likely to do so themselves. My own research also demonstrates that empathy is contagious: People "catch" one another's care and altruism. Here are a few ways leaders can leverage this insight to build empathy in their workplaces.

Acknowledge the potential for growth.
When people think of empathy as a trait that one either has or doesn't have, it may seem out of reach. If you can't learn something, why bother trying? Carol Dweck, Karina Schumman, and I have found that people with this kind of "fixed mindset" around empathy work less hard to connect with others.[2] If such beliefs permeate an organization, encouraging empathy as a collective value will fall flat.

The good news is that our mindsets can change. In a follow-up study as part of the research I mentioned above, my coauthors and I presented people with evidence that empathy is less like a trait and more like a skill.[3] They responded by working harder at it, even when it didn't come naturally. In other words, the first step toward building empathy is acknowledging that *it can be built*. Leaders should start by assessing the mindsets of their employees and teaching them that they can indeed move toward their ideals.

Highlight the right norms.
The loudest voices are seldom the kindest, but when they dominate conversations they can also hijack our perceptions. Hard-partying college freshmen brag about their weekend exploits, and as a result

Idea in Brief

The Research

Research shows that empathic workplaces tend to enjoy stronger collaboration, less stress, and greater morale, and their employees bounce back more quickly from difficult moments such as layoffs. Still, many leaders struggle to make caring part of their organizational culture.

The Path Forward

The first step toward building empathy is acknowledging that it's not an inherent trait but something that can be built. Watch out for "phantom norms"—behaviors that seem to be dominant just because a few prominent or loud individuals display them. Identify connectors—the people who encourage team cohesion even though it's not part of their formal role—and recruit them to champion the cause for empathy.

their peers conclude that the average student likes binge drinking more than they really do. When one team member loudly expresses a toxic attitude, colleagues can confuse that attitude for the majority opinion. Such "phantom norms" can derail positive change when people conform to them.

Leaders can fight back against phantom norms by drawing attention to the right behaviors. At any moment, some individuals in an organization are acting kindly while others are not. Some are working together while others are competing. Empathy often belongs to a quiet majority. Foregrounding it—for instance, through incentives and recognition—can allow employees to see its prevalence, turning up the volume on a positive norm.

Find culture leaders and co-create with them.

Every group, whether it's an NBA team, a corporate division, or a police department, includes people who encourage team cohesion even though it's not part of their formal role. These individuals might not be the most popular or powerful, but they are the most connected. Information, ideas, and values flow through them. They are their groups' unsung influencers.

In a recent study, Betsy Levy Paluck and her colleagues used this wisdom to change culture in middle schools.[4] They deputized students to create anti-bullying campaigns, which were then spread around campus. The student deputies varied in how socially well-connected they were. Levy Paluck found that peer-led anti-bullying campaigns worked, but they were especially effective when they were helmed by the most-connected students.

To build empathic cultures, leaders can begin by identifying connectors and recruiting them for help in championing the cause. This not only increases the likelihood that new ideals will "take," it also allows employees to be recognized for connecting with others—highlighting another positive social norm.

Empathy deserves its buzzy status, and leaders are wise to desire it for their businesses. But to succeed in making it part of their organization's DNA, they must pay close attention to how cultures build and change—organically, collectively, and often from the bottom up.

Reprinted from hbr.org, originally published May 30, 2019. Reprint HO4Z8H

Notes

1. "2023 State of Workplace Empathy Report," Businesssolver, https://www.businessolver.com/workplace-empathy/#gref.

2. K. Schumann, J. Zaki, and C. S. Dweck, "Addressing the Empathy Deficit: Beliefs about the Malleability of Empathy Predict Effortful Responses When Empathy Is Challenging," *Journal of Personality and Social Psychology* 107, no. 3 (2014): 475–493.

3. E. C. Nook, D. C. Ong, S. A. Morelli, J. P. Mitchell, and J. Zaki, "Prosocial Conformity: Prosocial Norms Generalize Across Behavior and Empathy," *Personal and Social Psychology Bulletin* 42, no. 8 (2016): 1045–1062.

4. E. L. Paluck, H. Shepherd, and P. M. Aronow, "Changing Climates of Conflict: A Social Network Experiment in 56 Schools," *Psychological and Cognitive Sciences* 113, no. 3 (January 2016): 566–571.

Learning to Learn

by Erika Andersen

ORGANIZATIONS TODAY ARE IN CONSTANT FLUX. Industries are consolidating, new business models are emerging, new technologies are being developed, and consumer behaviors are evolving. For executives, the ever-increasing pace of change can be especially demanding. It forces them to understand and quickly respond to big shifts in the way companies operate and how work must get done. In the words of Arie de Geus, a business theorist, "The ability to learn faster than your competitors may be the only sustainable competitive advantage."

I'm not talking about relaxed armchair or even structured classroom learning. I'm talking about resisting the bias against doing new things, scanning the horizon for growth opportunities, and pushing yourself to acquire radically different capabilities—while still performing your job. That requires a willingness to experiment and become a novice again and again: an extremely discomforting notion for most of us.

Over decades of coaching and consulting to thousands of executives in a variety of industries, however, my colleagues and I have come across people who succeed at this kind of learning. We've identified four attributes they have in spades: aspiration, self-awareness, curiosity, and vulnerability. They truly want to understand and master new skills; they see themselves very clearly; they constantly think of and ask good questions; and they tolerate their own mistakes as they move up the learning curve.

Of course, these things come more naturally to some people than to others. But, drawing on research in psychology and management as well as our work with clients, we have identified some fairly simple mental tools anyone can develop to boost all four attributes— even those that are often considered fixed (aspiration, curiosity, and vulnerability).

Aspiration

It's easy to see aspiration as either there or not: You want to learn a new skill or you don't; you have ambition and motivation or you lack them. But great learners can raise their aspiration level—and that's key, because everyone is guilty of sometimes resisting development that is critical to success.

Think about the last time your company adopted a new approach—overhauled a reporting system, replaced a CRM platform, revamped the supply chain. Were you eager to go along? I doubt it. Your initial response was probably to justify not learning. (*It will take too long. The old way works just fine for me. I bet it's just a flash in the pan.*) When confronted with new learning, this is often our first roadblock: We focus on the negative and unconsciously reinforce our lack of aspiration.

When we *do* want to learn something, we focus on the positive— what we'll gain from learning it—and envision a happy future in which we're reaping those rewards. That propels us into action. Researchers have found that shifting your focus from challenges to benefits is a good way to increase your aspiration to do initially unappealing things. For example, when Nicole Detling, a psychologist at the University of Utah, encouraged aerialists and speed skaters to picture themselves benefiting from a particular skill, they were much more motivated to practice it.

A few years ago I coached a CMO who was hesitant to learn about big data. Even though most of his peers were becoming converts, he'd convinced himself that he didn't have the time to get into it and that it wouldn't be that important to his industry. I finally realized

Idea in Brief

The ever-increasing pace of change in today's organizations requires that executives understand and then quickly respond to constant shifts in how their businesses operate and how work must get done. That means you must resist your innate biases against doing new things in new ways, scan the horizon for growth opportunities, and push yourself to acquire drastically different capabilities—while still doing your existing job. To succeed, you must be willing to experiment and become a novice over and over again, which for most of us is an extremely discomforting proposition.

Over decades of work with managers, the author has found that people who do succeed at this kind of learning have four well-developed attributes: aspiration, self-awareness, curiosity, and vulnerability. They have a deep desire to understand and master new skills; they see themselves very clearly; they're constantly thinking of and asking good questions; and they tolerate their own mistakes as they move up the curve. There are some fairly simple mental strategies that anyone can use to boost these attributes.

that this was an aspiration problem and encouraged him to think of ways that getting up to speed on data-driven marketing could help him personally. He acknowledged that it would be useful to know more about how various segments of his customer base were responding to his team's online advertising and in-store marketing campaigns. I then invited him to imagine the situation he'd be in a year later if he was getting that data. He started to show some excitement, saying, "We would be testing different approaches simultaneously, both in-store and online; we'd have good, solid information about which ones were working and for whom; and we could save a lot of time and money by jettisoning the less effective approaches faster." I could almost feel his aspiration rising. Within a few months he'd hired a data analytics expert, made a point of learning from her on a daily basis, and begun to rethink key campaigns in light of his new perspective and skills.

Self-Awareness

Over the past decade or so, most leaders have grown familiar with the concept of self-awareness. They understand that they need to solicit feedback and recognize how others see them. But when it comes to the need for learning, our assessments of ourselves—what we know and don't know, skills we have and don't have—can still be woefully inaccurate. In one study conducted by David Dunning, a Cornell University psychologist, 94% of college professors reported that they were doing "above average work." Clearly, almost half were wrong—many extremely so—and their self-deception surely diminished any appetite for development. Only 6% of respondents saw themselves as having a lot to learn about being an effective teacher.

In my work I've found that the people who evaluate themselves most accurately start the process inside their own heads: They accept that their perspective is often biased or flawed and then strive for greater objectivity, which leaves them much more open to hearing and acting on others' opinions. The trick is to pay attention to how you talk to yourself about yourself and then question the validity of that "self-talk."

Let's say your boss has told you that your team isn't strong enough and that you need to get better at assessing and developing talent. Your initial reaction might be something like *What? She's wrong. My team is strong.* Most of us respond defensively to that sort of criticism. But as soon as you recognize what you're thinking, ask yourself, *Is that accurate? What facts do I have to support it?* In the process of reflection you may discover that you're wrong and your boss is right, or that the truth lies somewhere in between—you cover for some of your reports by doing things yourself, and one of them is inconsistent in meeting deadlines; however, two others are stars. Your inner voice is most useful when it reports the facts of a situation in this balanced way. It should serve as a "fair witness" so that you're open to seeing the areas in which you could improve and how to do so.

One CEO I know was convinced that he was a great manager and leader. He did have tremendous industry knowledge and great

Changing your inner narrative

Unsupportive self-talk	Supportive self-talk
I don't need to learn this.	What would my future look like if I did?
I'm already fine at this.	Am I really? How do I compare with my peers?
This is boring.	I wonder why others find it interesting.
I'm terrible at this.	I'm making beginner mistakes, but I'll get better.

instincts about growing his business, and his board acknowledged those strengths. But he listened only to people who affirmed his view of himself and dismissed input about shortcomings; his team didn't feel engaged or inspired. When he finally started to question his assumptions (*Is everyone on my team focused and productive? If not, is there something I could be doing differently?*), he became much more aware of his developmental needs and open to feedback. He realized that it wasn't enough to have strategic insights; he had to share them with his reports and invite discussion, and then set clear priorities—backed by quarterly team and individual goals, regular progress checks, and troubleshooting sessions.

Curiosity

Kids are relentless in their urge to learn and master. As John Medina writes in *Brain Rules,* "This need for explanation is so powerfully stitched into their experience that some scientists describe it as a drive, just as hunger and thirst and sex are drives." Curiosity is what makes us try something until we can do it, or think about something until we understand it. Great learners retain this childhood drive, or regain it through another application of self-talk. Instead of focusing on and reinforcing initial disinterest in a new subject, they learn to ask themselves "curious questions" about it and follow those questions up with actions. Carol Sansone, a psychology researcher, has found, for example, that people can increase their willingness to tackle necessary tasks by thinking about how they could do the work differently to make it more interesting. In other words, they change their self-talk from *This is boring* to *I wonder if I could . . . ?*

You can employ the same strategy in your working life by noticing the language you use in thinking about things that already interest you—*How . . . ? Why . . . ? I wonder . . . ?*—and drawing on it when you need to become curious. Then take just one step to answer a question you've asked yourself: Read an article, query an expert, find a teacher, join a group—whatever feels easiest.

I recently worked with a corporate lawyer whose firm had offered her a bigger job that required knowledge of employment law—an area she regarded as "the single most boring aspect of the legal profession." Rather than trying to persuade her otherwise, I asked her what she was curious about and why. "Swing dancing," she said. "I'm fascinated by the history of it. I wonder how it developed, and whether it was a response to the Depression—it's such a happy art form. I watch great dancers and think about why they do certain things."

I explained that her "curious language" could be applied to employment law. "I wonder how anyone could find it interesting?" she said jokingly. I told her that was actually an OK place to start. She began thinking out loud about possible answers ("Maybe some lawyers see it as a way to protect both their employees and their companies . . .") and then proposed a few other curious questions ("How might knowing more about this make me a better lawyer?").

Soon she was intrigued enough to connect with a colleague who was experienced in employment law. She asked him what he found interesting about it and how he had acquired his knowledge, and his answers prompted other questions. Over the following months she learned what she needed to know for that aspect of her new role.

The next time you're asked to learn something at the office, or sense that you should because colleagues are doing so, encourage yourself to ask and answer a few curious questions about it—*Why are others so excited about this? How might this make my job easier?*—and then seek out the answers. You'll need to find just one thing about a "boring" topic that sparks your curiosity.

Vulnerability

Once we become good or even excellent at some things, we rarely want to go back to being *not* good at other things. Yes, we're now taught to embrace experimentation and "fast failure" at work. But we're also taught to play to our strengths. So the idea of being bad at something for weeks or months; feeling awkward and slow; having to ask "dumb," "I-don't-know-what-you're-talking-about" questions; and needing step-by-step guidance again and again is extremely scary. Great learners allow themselves to be vulnerable enough to accept that beginner state. In fact, they become reasonably comfortable in it—by managing their self-talk.

Generally, when we're trying something new and doing badly at it, we think terrible thoughts: *I hate this. I'm such an idiot. I'll never get this right. This is so frustrating!* That static in our brains leaves little bandwidth for learning. The ideal mindset for a beginner is both vulnerable and balanced: *I'm going to be bad at this to start with, because I've never done it before. AND I know I can learn to do it over time.* In fact, the researchers Robert Wood and Albert Bandura found in the late 1980s that when people are encouraged to expect mistakes and learn from them early in the process of acquiring new skills, the result is "heightened interest, persistence, and better performance."

I know a senior sales manager from the United States who was recently tapped to run the Asia-Pacific region for his company. He was having a hard time acclimating to living overseas and working with colleagues from other cultures, and he responded by leaning on his sales expertise rather than acknowledging his beginner status in the new environment. I helped him recognize his resistance to being a cultural novice, and he was able to shift his self-talk from *This is so uncomfortable—I'll just focus on what I already know* to *I have a lot to learn about Asian cultures. I'm a quick study, so I'll be able to pick it up.* He told me it was an immediate relief: Simply acknowledging his novice status made him feel less foolish and more relaxed. He started asking the necessary questions, and soon he was seen as open, interested, and beginning to understand his new environment.

––––––––––––

The ability to acquire new skills and knowledge quickly and continually is crucial to success in a world of rapid change. If you don't currently have the aspiration, self-awareness, curiosity, and vulnerability to be an effective learner, these simple tools can help you get there.

Originally published in March 2016. Reprint R1603J

How to Get the Help You Need

by Heidi Grant

FEW OF US enjoy asking for help. As research in neuroscience and psychology shows, the social threats involved—the uncertainty, risk of rejection, potential for diminished status, and inherent relinquishing of autonomy—activate the same brain regions that physical pain does. And in the workplace, where we're typically keen to demonstrate as much expertise, competence, and confidence as possible, it can feel particularly uncomfortable to make such requests.

However, it's virtually impossible to advance in modern organizations without assistance from others. Cross-functional teams, agile project management techniques, matrixed or hierarchy-minimizing structures, and increasingly collaborative office cultures require you to constantly push for the cooperation and support of your managers, peers, and employees. Your performance, development, and career progression depend more than ever on your seeking out the advice, referrals, and resources you need. In fact, estimates suggest that as much as 75% to 90% of the help coworkers give one another is in response to direct appeals.

So how can you effectively ask for help? How can you impose upon people without making them feel imposed upon?

The first step is getting over your reluctance to ask for assistance. Next, you need to understand that some common and perhaps intuitive ways of asking for help are ultimately unproductive, because they make people less likely to want to give it. Finally, you must learn the subtle cues that motivate people to support you and how to deliver them in the right way.

Costs and Benefits

Perhaps the easiest way to overcome the pain of asking for help is to realize that most people are surprisingly willing to lend a hand. When Vanessa Bohns, a professor at Cornell University and a leading researcher in this area, recently reviewed a group of experiments that she and her coauthors had done, she found that compliance—the rate at which people provided assistance to strangers who asked for it—was an average of 48% higher than the help seekers had expected. Clearly, people are much more likely to be helpful than we think they are. Studies also suggest that we underestimate how much effort those who do agree to help will put in.

That's in part because saying no or helping only halfheartedly carries a psychological cost that we tend to discount. But it's also because most helpers know—even if only subconsciously—that giving freely and effectively of themselves has emotional benefits. A Swiss study published in 2017 found that people who simply pledge to spend even a small amount of money on someone else feel happier than those who plan to indulge only themselves.

The key to a successful request for help is to shift the focus to these benefits. You want people to feel that they would be helping because they want to, not because they must, and that they're in control of the decision. That means avoiding any language suggesting that you or someone else is instructing them to help, that they should help, or that they have no choice but to do so. This includes prefaces such as "May I ask you a favor?" which make people feel trapped, and profuse apologies such as "I feel terrible asking you for this," which make the experience seem less positive. Emphasizing reciprocity—"I'll help you if you help me"—can also backfire, because people don't like to be indebted to anyone or to engage in a purely transactional exchange. And minimizing your need—"I don't normally ask for help" or "It's just a tiny thing"—is

Idea in Brief

The Problem

We're often reluctant to ask for help because of the social threats involved—uncertainty, risk of rejection, potential for diminished status, relinquishment of authority. But without support from others, it's virtually impossible to advance in your career. And studies show that most people are surprisingly willing to lend a hand—if you ask in the right way.

The Solution

Three reinforcements can be incorporated in requests for help:

- **In-group:** Assure the potential helper that you are on the same team and that the team is important.

- **Positive identity:** Create or enhance people's recognition that they are uniquely placed to provide assistance and that they routinely come to others' aid.

- **Effectiveness:** Be clear about what you need and about what impact the help will have.

---

equally unproductive, because it suggests the assistance is trivial or even unnecessary.

But you can ask for help in a way that avoids these pitfalls and instead gives people agency over their responses, allowing them to experience the natural highs associated with helping. That's by using what I call reinforcements, or cues, which you can incorporate in specific requests. Perhaps more important, you can also use them in day-to-day interactions to prime the people around you for greater helpfulness.

Three Reinforcements

In-group.

One reinforcement you'll want to give a potential helper is assurance that you're on their team and that the team is important. This taps into the innate human need to belong to—and ensure the well-being of—supportive social circles. There are several ways to do this. For example, research by Priyanka Carr and Greg Walton (a graduate student at the time), of Stanford University, shows that simply saying the word "together" can have an effect. When participants working on puzzles alone were told that they were doing so in tandem with people performing similar tasks in other rooms and could later exchange tips, they worked 48% longer, solved more problems correctly, and said they were less depleted by the task than those allowed to believe they were working fully independently.

You might also cite a common goal, enemy, or trait, such as the desire to exceed your team's sales targets, rivalry with a competitor in your industry, or a love of superhero movies. But the best way to create a strong sense of in-group is to highlight shared experiences, perceptions, thoughts, and feelings. For example, if a senior management team includes only two women, don't just say, "We're the only two women on the team" (emphasizing the trait). Say, "Have you noticed that we get interrupted all the time?" (shared experience).

Positive identity.
A second cue for potential helpers involves creating or enhancing their recognition that they are uniquely placed (by virtue of their attributes or role) to provide assistance and that they are not merely people who might help you but helpful people who routinely come to others' aid. For example, studies have shown that people contribute more to charity when asked if they would like to "be a generous donor" (versus "to donate") and that children as young as three are more motivated to complete tasks such as cleaning up blocks when told they can "be a helper" (versus "can help"). Remember, however, that people don't all have the same vision of positive identity, so tailor your message. Research on pro-environment appeals suggests, for instance, that liberals prefer phrases such as "care for the natural world" and "prevent the suffering of all life forms," whereas conservatives respond better to "show your love for your country" and "take responsibility for yourself and the land you call home."

Gratitude is another powerful way to boost helpers' positive identity. A recent study by the productivity software company Boomerang of 350,000 email exchanges found that "Thanks in advance" and "Thanks" yielded average response rates from 63% to

66%, compared with 51% to 54% for other popular options including "Best," "Regards," and "Cheers." Even expressed preemptively, gratitude can keep people interested and invested in helping you, as long as you focus more on their generosity and selflessness—and what that says about them as people—than on how you'll benefit from the help.

Effectiveness.

People want to see or know the impact of the aid they will give. This isn't an ego thing. Many psychologists believe that feeling effective—knowing that your actions created the results you intended—is the fundamental human motivation; it's what truly engages people and gives their lives meaning. Consider a study that Wharton's Adam Grant conducted at an outbound call center in an educational and marketing software company. Employees knew that the revenue they generated supported jobs in another department, with which they'd previously had no contact. After one of the beneficiaries of their work visited and spoke to them about their impact on his and others' jobs, the call center's sales and revenue doubled. To ensure that your potential helpers know that their assistance will matter, be very clear about what you need and its projected impact. For example, when asking a colleague to review a client proposal, you might say, "Would you please review this before I send it to XYZ? Your input really helped my previous pitch to ABC succeed."

Promise to follow up afterward, and do so. If possible, also allow people to choose how they help you, and be willing to accept alternatives to your original request. You want helpers to give what they can—and what will make them feel most effective.

Personal and Professional

When I explain to people how these strategies work in practice, I often give an example from my personal life, involving an IKEA bookshelf. About a year ago, a friend from graduate school asked me to help her assemble a particularly complicated one, and—this might surprise you—I eagerly agreed. That same morning, I'd turned down a request to review a submission to a scientific journal, ignored an email from my daughter's school asking for parent volunteers to help with an ice cream party, and grudgingly said I would do our family's laundry but refused to fold it. So why was the DIY request an easy yes?

One reason is that the person asking was a long-standing friend with whom I enjoy spending time (*in-group* reinforcement). Another is that I'm weirdly good at such projects (owing less to my construction prowess than to my ability to interpret poorly written directions), and for years I'd been her go-to gal for help with them (*effectiveness*). And finally, whenever we work together in this way, my friend always wraps up by saying something like "Heidi, thank you. You are always so helpful and generous" (*positive identity*).

I've seen situations play out the same way in professional settings. Consider the head of product development at a learning software company who wanted more input with the sales department, which was making his team's work difficult by agreeing that highly customized orders would be delivered according to near-impossible schedules. He pleaded to be included in discussions with clients but was often ignored; the people in sales believed that he would slow them down and be an obstacle to their success. Of course, all parties felt they were doing what was best for the company, but in their own ways.

Eventually, the frustrated executive decided to take a fresh approach to getting the cooperation he needed from his colleagues. He set up a meeting with sales leaders to talk through the product development process, realizing that most of the team had no idea what work was involved. In other words, they didn't understand why their help was needed. He began to emphasize in every interaction that they all shared the goal of pleasing the customer to ensure repeat business, creating a strong sense of *in-group* with the sales team. Suddenly it was clear that everyone was on the same side. He also started describing sales leaders as the protectors of customer experience and talked about the power they wielded in determining the future of the company's brand, which gave them a strong *positive identity* and motivated them to see and approach their work in a slightly different way.

What Helpers Need

1. **The helper must realize that you need help.** Human beings are, as a rule, preoccupied with their own affairs. This is particularly true for people in negative moods or positions of relative power over others. So the first step is making people aware of your problem.

2. **The helper must believe that you want help.** Sometimes people fail to offer help not because they don't see the need but because they're worried that they've misconstrued the situation or that you prefer to go it alone. They expect you to come to them, forgetting how reluctant most of us are to ask for help.

3. **The helper must take responsibility for helping.** One of the biggest obstacles to helping is diffusion of responsibility. A classic error is asking for help via group email. Instead take the time to ask potential helpers directly and with unique appeals.

4. **The helper must be able to provide what you need.** People are busy, and not all of them have the skills or the resources to help you. But you can make any request seem more manageable by being explicit and detailed about what you are asking for, keeping the request reasonable, and staying open to receiving help that is different from what you asked for.

Finally, whenever salespeople did what he asked and included him in the work proposal process, he made a point of following up with them to say how important it had been to the ultimate success of the delivery. They saw their help land and felt its *effectiveness*.

Over time, these strategies dramatically improved relations between the two teams, and the company saw increases in both client satisfaction and profitability.

When you next find yourself in need of help, remember that people are willing to give it much more often than not. Few will think less of you for needing assistance. And there is no better way to make someone feel good about themselves than to ask for it. It brings out the best—and the best feelings—in all of us.

Originally published in May–June 2018. Reprint R1803M

How to Sell Your Ideas up the Chain of Command

by Ethan Burris

YOU HAVE A great idea—a product tweak that will save your company money, a process change to increase your team's productivity, or a plan for heading off a looming crisis. There's just one snag: You're not sure how to approach your boss about it, or worse, you've tried and failed to get the attention of higher-ups.

Despite abundant research on the value of bottom-up innovation and problem-solving, many workers still feel stifled in giving their bosses feedback or making suggestions. One survey of U.S. employees found that a full 70% weren't comfortable raising an issue with their boss even when it was important, and a landmark 2003 study found that 85% of employees withheld their ideas because they were afraid to speak up.

Additional research shows that even when employees do speak up, their suggestions usually don't lead to change. For example, an Accenture study showed that nearly three-fourths of ideas submitted through corporate online suggestion tools languished and were never implemented. Another study of a hospital found that of 200 ideas shared by employees, most were initially rejected and fewer than a quarter were ever implemented.

For the past two decades, I've studied how employees offer solicited and unsolicited recommendations and how managers respond.

Obviously, there are many reasons why ideas—including those from senior leaders—fail to make it to implementation. But too often good ideas are ignored or rejected. I've found that two factors are key to a successful pitch: having the confidence to make your suggestion and knowing how to frame it to get the best reception from your boss. Some managers will be more unapproachable and unresponsive than others, but research shows that the majority are more open to ideas and suggestions than you might imagine—provided they are approached effectively.

In the studies my colleagues and I have conducted across health care, restaurant, oil and gas, technology, and financial service organizations, we've uncovered several strategies that you can use to make yourself heard by managers, thereby enhancing both your company's performance and your own experience at work. We've found that the key to selling your idea up the chain of command is to understand the psychology of higher-ups—to get inside their heads. Doing so can help you recognize what tips the scales in your favor—and identify the (rare) instances when it's best to try to go around or above them.

Understand Your Manager's Insecurities

When deciding whether to speak up about an idea or a problem at work, most employees think first about their own standing. Do I want to risk the potential embarrassment of being rejected by the boss? Will my manager see me as a complainer, a worrywart, or a pot-stirrer? Few people, however, focus on their manager's ego. How will this suggestion make my boss feel?

Being the boss comes with heavy expectations. Leaders are supposed to be well-informed and know what to do all or most of the time. That can make them feel insecure and leave them less open to subordinates' ideas. Consider the survey we did of highly educated managers—chemists, geologists, geophysicists, petroleum and environmental engineers, drillers, and executive staff—at a multinational oil and gas company. We found that despite being exceedingly accomplished, many lacked confidence in their ability to lead. In

Idea in Brief

The Problem

You have a great idea—a product tweak that will save your company money, a process change to increase your team's productivity, or a plan for heading off a looming crisis. There's just one snag: You're not sure how to approach your boss about it, or worse, you've tried and failed to get the attention of higher-ups.

The Solution

According to research, two factors are crucial to a successful pitch:

having the confidence to make your suggestion and knowing how to frame it to get the best reception from your boss. The key is to understand the psychology of higher-ups—to get inside their heads. Doing so can help you recognize what tips the scales in your favor—and identify the (rare) instances when it's best to try to go around or above them.

another study, we found that with each one-point decrease in confidence on a five-point scale, managers were 35% less likely to solicit advice from their employees. And a follow-up study of more than 130 managers across industries showed that insecure managers gave workers who spoke up evaluations that were 21% more negative—and implemented their ideas 14% less frequently—than managers who felt more comfortable in their roles did.

Of course, some leaders are able to absorb feedback and ideas without feeling criticized or threatened. But even in those cases, there is very little downside to protecting their egos and neutralizing their insecurities. And it's possible to do so without feeling manipulative or sycophantic or exerting a lot of effort.

Ideally, when you propose an idea to higher-ups, you'll have already laid the groundwork by building trust and goodwill. Giving your manager positive feedback and expressing gratitude can help in this regard, provided the sentiments are genuine and delivered long before your pitch. It can be something as simple as, "I really enjoyed that presentation" or "Thanks for your support in the meeting today."

As research by Adam Grant, Sharon Parker, and Catherine Collins has shown, managers pay attention to whether their employees tend to help themselves or help others. By routinely supporting your peers, you send signals that your suggestions are designed to improve the organization as a whole—and your manager's standing. Indeed, explicitly conveying the benevolence of your motives can be helpful when making a suggestion to your boss, according to research led by Harvard Business School's Leslie John. Especially when you're giving negative feedback, prefacing your comments with a simple phrase such as "I really want the best for you" can help you avoid the likability penalty often paid by messengers of bad news.

When possible, approach your manager in private rather than publicly. A study by Sofya Isaakyan of the Rotterdam School of Management and colleagues showed that managers felt 30% less threatened when employees spoke to them one-on-one than when the suggestions were made in front of other employees.

Finally, try to frame your suggestions in a way that links them to the company's stated goals. You might reference your boss's previous communications: for example, "You've spoken before about your focus on intuitive design. Here's my idea for improving the user-friendliness of X product" or "I was thinking back to that email you sent about the importance of diversity, equity, and inclusion and wondering if we could make more progress by shifting our recruitment efforts from Y to Z."

Avoid Mixed Messages

When selling an idea, people often frame it by combining two messages: the benefits of doing something new and the risk of inaction. This is a mistake. Across five studies with executives from dozens of industries, my colleagues and I learned that managers are more likely to endorse messages that focus on either an opportunity or a threat; a combination of the two garners the least support.

In one of the studies, we analyzed more than 850 ideas submitted by 350 employees in a hospital system in the Midwest. They included suggestions about how to improve staff satisfaction, quality of care, patient satisfaction, and patient safety. We found that when proposals referenced both an opportunity and a threat, managers had to exert more effort to understand the nature and severity of the problem, the solution, and why the proposal was better than the status quo. The increased cognitive work brought additional scrutiny and colored how managers evaluated those ideas, often leading to their rejection. On the flip side, proposals that used one frame were more likely to be endorsed.

Which frame should you use? Our research revealed that employees should try to discern whether the managers they're pitching to have a "promotion focus" (that is, they focus on aspirations, ideals, the future, and playing to win) or a "prevention focus" (they're preoccupied with staying vigilant, managing downsides, and playing not to lose) and then frame proposals accordingly.

A promotion-focused manager will want to know that an idea presents a new and exciting opportunity with tremendous upside. A prevention-focused manager will need to know how the suggestion will help the team avoid a problem or loss. Our research across several studies involving more than 800 frontline managers shows that tailoring the message to a manager's personality can increase the likelihood that an idea will be endorsed by 15% to 18%.

There is no surefire way to diagnose your manager's focus, but most people have tells. Is your boss concerned with obeying rules, following standard operating procedures, and upholding company policy? Very careful in outlining and executing on plans? Meticulous with the details of work and not messing anything up? If so, he probably has a prevention focus. Or does your manager like to start projects but doesn't necessarily finish them all? Does she talk often about what the future holds? Prefer that others worry about the details of projects? Let little mistakes slide? If so, she most likely has a promotion focus.

Make Implementation Easy

Even when managers see the merit in an idea, there's no guarantee they'll back it amid myriad challenges and competing priorities. So it's helpful to anticipate potential obstacles and explain how they might be overcome. In studies of a large hospital ER, a commercial real estate firm, and a defense contracting company, we found that managers typically evaluated an employee-generated idea by considering three questions: What financial and human resources will be required to implement it? How difficult will it be to enlist the help of others? Is it worth devoting time, energy, and political capital to? You'll want to address all three areas of concern in your pitch.

Consider a cautionary tale of a physician who suggested that ER patient flow could be managed more effectively by using additional nurses to triage patients. While the benefits would be substantial (for example, patients would receive critical care more quickly), the costs would most likely be steep: The proposal could require additional head count, present scheduling challenges, and cause shortages of skilled staff in other areas of the hospital, such as the ICU and operating rooms. The physician hadn't thought enough about those hurdles before speaking to his manager, and so the idea was quickly shot down. A nurse we talked to shared a similar story. She proposed a better system for dealing with psychiatric and intoxicated patients who were overburdening her ER, but because the plan required coordination with various external groups—police, social services, policy makers, and others, each of which had different contacts within the hospital—her boss couldn't see a way to make it happen. If she had thought through how those relationships might be managed, her proposal would probably have gotten more traction.

In contrast, another physician who kept management concerns in mind in presenting a potential solution to a problem was more successful. Because his hospital was the only Level 1 trauma center in the region, it attracted a lot of distracting media attention, from reporters covering sensational injuries to photographers capturing local celebrities getting treatment. Managers, nurses, and doctors had to spend valuable time away from their health care duties dealing with the news outlets. Instead of suggesting that the hospital hire additional public relations staff or create a costly and complicated process for handling the media, the doctor made one simple suggestion: erect a privacy barrier at the ambulance entrance, preventing the media from seeing arriving patients. This cost a few thousand dollars, required zero staff time, and saved the hospital a lot of headaches.

So before you approach higher-ups, give some thought to the potential challenges to execution. You might end up scrapping your idea—but generally, thinking about obstacles will strengthen your case. In making your pitch, describe how budgets and people could be redeployed to your idea without putting undue stress on other projects or parts of the business. Discuss which allies you'd need to enlist, and volunteer to help bring them on board. And don't forget to highlight how your idea aligns with the organization's values and strategy—and why supporting it is worthwhile for your manager.

For example, an employee trying to persuade the boss to let the team continue to work remotely postpandemic might focus on the economic advantages (such as real estate cost savings) if she knows her company is particularly focused on running a tight P&L. Or if the organization and its leaders tout their commitment to staff wellness and work/life balance and reward bosses who drive engagement by promoting such efforts, she might emphasize the benefits of eliminating workers' long commutes. By tapping into the key values of the company—which are often reflected in the specific measures on which your manager is evaluated—you can better frame your ideas to make them seem more worthy of action. Indeed, a study led by David Mayer showed that in values-driven organizations, employees who talked about company values when advocating for an idea were 24% more successful than those who didn't.

Leverage Colleagues

Employees often fail to seek guidance or support from coworkers before offering feedback and suggestions. In one study I conducted, nearly 60% of people talked directly to their managers before running ideas by colleagues to see if they had merit. This is striking, given that the first question managers ask themselves is often whether the issue is a big deal affecting many stakeholders—or the employee is being overly enthusiastic or a "squeaky wheel."

Many voices are obviously more persuasive than just one, and allies give you credibility. Before approaching your boss, share your thoughts with your coworkers, take counsel on how to improve your pitch, and ask if you can mention their support or if they'd be willing to join you in presenting the idea. Across several studies, employees who amplified the voices of others in their pitches were 15% to 20% more influential than those who spoke only on their own behalf.

You might even consider asking a well-positioned coworker to present your idea for you. A colleague who has more domain expertise or a better relationship with your boss might be more persuasive than you would be. Even better if you can choose someone who won't directly benefit from the change; such a person's arguments are likely to be seen as more legitimate. After all, your colleague is sticking their neck out for you. In a forthcoming study, my coauthors and I found that people who spoke up on behalf of others were 57% more influential than those who spoke up for themselves.

Joining forces with colleagues has yet another benefit—it helps diffuse any knee-jerk frustration that the manager might take out on the person making the suggestion. Research by Leslie John has found that people are prone to disparaging those who tell them things they don't want to hear—that is, they shoot the messenger. There's safety in numbers, so enlist some allies.

Pitch to the Right Person

Putting yourself in your manager's shoes will also make you more likely to identify the instances when they *can't* help. It is pointless to continually raise issues with a boss who lacks the power or authority to address them. For example, one restaurant employee spoke to his shift manager about the lower wages earned by people who'd been at the company for years compared with those earned by much-less-experienced workers. He quickly realized that his boss had no control over compensation policy; corporate HR did, and by bringing the matter up to the wrong person, he was more likely to cause frustration than inspire positive change.

In such cases, consider what's in your managers' purview and whether other managers would be better targets for your suggestions. Who has the decision rights? Is it human resources? Facilities? Your manager's manager? If it's unclear who the right person is, you might try using formal grievance systems or digital suggestion boxes to help you get your ideas out there.

To be clear, I'm not recommending that you simply go around your boss when you think they can't or won't take action. This is ill-advised in most cases—especially in highly political, top-down organizations or if your manager is particularly sensitive. A much better approach is to enlist your boss as an ally in selling your idea to the right department or up the chain of command. Approach your manager as a collaborator and coconspirator, and ask for help in crafting your suggestion in a way that will resonate with more-senior executives.

In spreading the word, try to find opportunities for informal conversations with higher-ups. As in-office activity resumes, seek them out in the cafeteria, on the elevator, at the holiday party. Bosses who might balk at an employee's scheduling a meeting to discuss an issue are likely to find impromptu chats less intimidating or even noteworthy.

Despite the clear benefits, innovation rarely bubbles up from below at most organizations. However, blame for those missed opportunities doesn't always lie with management. To sell your ideas up the chain of command, think about the psychology behind managers' resistance and reframe your proposals in a way that makes you a more persuasive advocate for change.

Originally published in January–February 2022. Reprint R2201L

When Diversity Meets Feedback

by Erin Meyer

IF YOU'VE PICKED UP A BOOK ABOUT raising organizational performance in the past five years, you've almost certainly read about the benefits of developing a culture of candid feedback. Kim Scott, a former Google executive, popularized the term "radical candor" in her 2017 book by that name, arguing that even "obnoxiously aggressive" feedback was better than "ruinous empathy" (keeping feedback that could otherwise help colleagues to yourself).

The hedge fund billionaire and Bridgewater founder Ray Dalio went a step further in his book *Principles,* describing a culture of "radical transparency," in which employees rate and give feedback about one another's contributions to meetings on publicly shared documents as the meetings actually take place. And in his 2020 book *No Rules Rules* (which I coauthored), Reed Hastings, Netflix's founder and executive chairman, lists candid feedback as one of the top three ingredients of an innovative organization. A popular motto at Netflix is "Only say about someone what you will say to their face." If an employee comes to the boss to complain about another employee, the boss is to respond, "What did your colleague say when you gave them that feedback?"

Most employees also recognize the benefits of frank and honest feedback, and they say they want more of it. In a 2019 survey by Zenger Folkman, 94% of 2,700 respondents said they believed corrective feedback improved their performance when it was presented well, while nearly two-thirds agreed with the statement "My performance and possibilities for success in my career would have increased substantially if I had been given more feedback." The survey's authors conclude that feedback—done right—can truly be a gift to individuals and organizations.

But there's another movement in business that has increasingly gained steam: diversity, equity, and inclusion. Bolstered by the Black Lives Matter and #MeToo movements, DEI is perhaps the most overarching organizational culture trend of the decade. Today every single *Fortune* 100 company cites DEI as a key priority on its website.

At first glance, DEI seems compatible with a culture of honest feedback. The more diverse the workforce, the more beneficial it is to hear everyone's opinions, and the more we all succeed. When Satya Nadella took over Microsoft, in 2014, he declared that he would work to turn what had become a know-it-all culture into a learn-it-all culture. While know-it-alls are focused on raising their status by showing off their expertise and hiding their weaknesses, learn-it-alls have the courage and humility to listen openly to constructive criticism and are eager to hear the opinions of teammates who have diverse viewpoints.

Unfortunately, a learn-it-all culture doesn't arise naturally. And when it comes to sharing feedback and advice, diversity often leads to complications, which, if not understood and managed, can create an environment rife with bad feelings, defensiveness, and ruptured relationships. That's because the vast majority of people aren't ready to receive criticism unless they feel safe with the person providing it. Do the people assessing your work really mean to help you, or are they surreptitiously trying to embarrass you, take your job, or usurp your power?

Diversity in the workplace, in fact, increases the likelihood that people will interpret feedback as an act of hostility. That means that people must be careful about how they provide it. Of course, diversity at work today encompasses many types of differences, from race and sexual orientation to religious and ethnic background. In the following pages I'll focus on how people can improve the way they

Idea in Brief

The Challenge

In recent years leading executives have touted the advantages of a work environment marked by candid feedback. Employees seem to have bought in to the benefits too. Unfortunately, the increased diversity of our workplaces has made it much more likely that feedback won't go over well and will be misinterpreted as an act of hostility. That's because people from different cultures, genders, and generations have varying expectations for how feedback is delivered and by whom.

The Path Forward

This article explains how to navigate the divides: Understand the norms of feedback for different recipients and adjust for them. Follow the three A's—make sure any advice is intended to *assist*, *is actionable*, and is *asked for*. Finally, get everyone on your team on the same page by establishing a common approach and building regular feedback loops into your collaborations.

deliver feedback across three specific types of diversity: cultures, genders, and generations. I'll also describe strategies for fostering a climate in which candor and diversity can coexist. I'll conclude by looking at how organizational practices can make frequent and regular feedback a standard part of working life.

1. Feedback Across Cultures: Upgrade, Downgrade, or Wrap Positives Around Negatives

In today's interconnected, virtual world you might have a strategy meeting with a colleague in India at 9 a.m., attend a financial presentation in Stockholm at 10, and run a program for new managers across South America at noon. If you're on a team that emphasizes candid feedback, at any moment of the day you may find yourself giving criticism to—or receiving it from—people from a wide variety of cultures and countries.

The risk of upsetting people in these situations is high. That's because what's considered a constructive way to offer feedback in one culture is often perceived as destructive in another. It isn't easy

Alarm Bells in the Brain

GIVING FEEDBACK IS TRICKY EVEN before factoring in the complications that arise from diversity, as an experiment I did with more than 3,000 executives who were my students at INSEAD shows. In it I presented them with a simple multiple-choice problem.

The Situation

You go to a meeting with a customer and a teammate. The teammate is senior to you but isn't your boss. You're friendly but not close. In the meeting your colleague speaks too loudly and is too intense. Your customer, a reserved person, responds with evident discomfort. When your customer speaks, your teammate often doesn't look at her, giving the impression that he isn't taking her seriously. When the meeting is over, will you give this feedback to your colleague?

Your Options

A. Yes. I'll give it clearly and quickly. It will help him, the client, and the organization.

B. Maybe. He hasn't asked for feedback. I'm not his boss, so it's not my responsibility. I'll wait and see if the right opportunity arises.

C. No. Unless he asks me, I won't provide it. I don't know if he is open to it, and I don't want to risk hurting our relationship.

In my research, more than 90% of participants chose option A, giving the feedback. This was consistent across industries, genders, cultural

for outsiders to understand the nuances around feedback in other cultures. For example, people across the world most often stereotype American culture as exceedingly direct. In some aspects this stereotype is true. Americans tend to place a high value on clear, simple communication and on actions like recapping key points and confirming decisions in writing. This approach certainly feels straightforward to many. But the story changes when it comes to negative feedback, whether in a critical performance review or an evaluation of a colleague's less-than-ideal presentation.

In those situations Americans tend to place an especially strong emphasis on preserving the self-esteem of the feedback recipient, backgrounds, and job levels. Surprised, I began asking a follow-up question: "What about your teammates? Would they provide the feedback?" This led to reflection and often laughter. Overwhelmingly, participants responded, "No. My teammates would clearly not provide the feedback."

(Follow-up comments included things like "In fact, I never receive any feedback at all, except occasionally from my boss.")

This prompted me to tease them, asking, "Isn't it interesting that only those rare people who would provide the feedback participate in my sessions?" Apparently, most managers, when faced with this problem in a classroom, say they'll give the feedback, but in real life they don't.

The issue is that the scenario triggers a conflict in people's brains between the frontal cortex and the amygdala. The cortex, the most logical part of the brain, loves candid feedback. But the brain's most primitive part, the amygdala, doesn't.

If you tell me I've acted ineffectively, it may trigger an alarm in my amygdala: "Danger! I might get kicked out of my tribe!" The stress hormones cortisol and adrenaline flood my bloodstream, throwing my body into "fight or flight" mode. The fight reaction leads me to respond defensively: "I'm not the problem. You are!" The flight reaction may result in a comment like "Thanks so much for that feedback. That is very helpful," after which I try to never speak to you again.

The challenge with feedback, therefore, is to make sure that your delivery succeeds in helping the cortex override the amygdala.

leading to common American practices such as giving three positives for every negative, catching people doing things right, and using superlatives to accentuate the positive, even when the negative is the key point. ("Overall it was excellent. To this part you might want to make some small tweaks.") This is downright confusing for people in countries where managers are much more likely to tell it like it is (the Netherlands, Germany, Denmark, Israel, Russia, and France—where I live—to name just a few).

A case in point is Olga, a Ukrainian human resource executive who attended my course at INSEAD. "In my culture if there is a problem, we say it clearly," Olga explained. "We don't perceive it as demotivating or unkind to say to a colleague, 'This is not OK,' or 'This behavior must change.' We don't talk about what we liked and appreciated before getting to the point or start the conversation by talking about the weather. We jump to the issue at hand."

Olga hadn't given cultural differences a lot of thought until she moved from Ukraine to West Virginia. In her job there, she says, "My colleague Cathy was responsible for payroll. Each month when the paychecks went out, there were mistakes. It was causing frustration, so I invited her into my office and said, 'Cathy, this absolutely cannot continue. Your mistakes are creating big headaches.'"

Later, when the seasonal-employee manager emailed Olga privately to complain ("Unbelievable! Cathy got the amounts wrong yet again"), Olga replied all, copying Cathy so that she could see the manager's comments herself and responding, "You are right. This is completely unacceptable, and it won't happen again." To Olga's surprise, her boss stopped by to correct *her* behavior, which he referred to as "indelicate." He informed her that Cathy had been so upset, she had asked to change jobs. He explained that Olga should not be critical of someone's work when other people are copied on the communication. He also suggested she use "might" and "should" rather than "must" and "can't." For Olga, this was a cultural eye-opener.

The complexity doesn't stop there. Americans may be masters at wrapping positives around negatives, but in some less-direct cultures the explicitness of the American approach is still likely to be perceived as inappropriately blunt. Take Jethro, a soft-spoken but forthright American working in Silicon Valley. With little understanding of cultural differences, he soon found himself in trouble for giving feedback (by video) to coworkers in Thailand using methods common in the United States. HR in Bangkok responded by complaining that he was bullying his Thai colleagues.

Jethro describes the situation like this: "I'd thought carefully about how to provide the feedback. My comments (both verbal and then in writing) were specific, explaining what actions had led to positive results and which had been problematic, and then outlining clearly what my colleagues needed to do differently to improve client satisfaction."

The head of HR in Thailand had some feedback of her own, however. "The American tendency to give feedback by explicitly stating 'the area in need of improvement' already feels aggressive to a Thai recipient," she told Jethro. "To make things worse, Americans frequently end discussions by recapping key points in writing, which makes us feel that you don't trust us to do as we say or are trying to get us in trouble."

She explained that Jethro would have more success if instead of detailing what his Thai colleagues had done wrong, he praised what was good clearly and left out what was bad. If he was specific about the things that had worked well, he didn't need to comment on the negative aspects at all; the Thai employees would understand that he was not happy with what he hadn't mentioned. For example, when commenting on a presentation he'd just seen, he might say, "I especially liked the examples you gave in the presentation last week." He wouldn't need to say, "The examples from this morning's presentation were not very good." It would be implied clearly enough.

Jethro learned the same lesson Olga did: "I saw clearly that what is normal and appropriate feedback in my culture may come off as completely inappropriate somewhere else," he reflects.

One way to gauge what feedback works best in another culture is to listen carefully to the words chosen by your counterparts. People from more-direct cultures tend to use what linguists call "upgraders" when providing criticism. These are words that make criticism feel stronger—like "absolutely," "totally," or "completely." For example, "This is absolutely inappropriate" or "This is totally unprofessional." By contrast, more-indirect cultures use more "downgraders" when giving negative feedback. These are words that soften the criticism, such as "kind of," "a little," and "maybe."

Another type of downgrader is a deliberate understatement—for example, saying, "We are not quite there yet," when you really mean "This is nowhere close to complete," or saying, "This is just my opinion," when you really mean "I'm certain this is obvious to everyone."

With a little awareness, you can notice when you're using upgraders and downgraders and when those around you are and make slight adjustments to get the desired results. When it comes to providing feedback internationally, the message is not "Do unto others as you would have them do unto you" but "Do unto others as they would have done unto themselves."

2. Feedback Across Genders: Give the Gift of Power First

Cultural differences represent only a small part of diversity in the workplace. Gender differences add to the complexity. As a woman at a business school where over three-quarters of the faculty members are men, I began thinking early on about how gender affects when and how we share our opinions.

Research shows that leaders who are women, much more than their male counterparts, are expected to be warm and nice (traditionally seen as female traits) as well as competent and tough (traits traditionally expected from men and leaders). This line is difficult to walk, and women who provide frank negative feedback risk being perceived as combative. One 2020 study conducted at Stanford University demonstrated that while women and men are equally likely to be described as having technical ability, women are significantly more likely to be described as aggressive. That's why women who provide candid feedback risk being perceived as on the attack.

The dynamics are just as complicated but completely different for men. In 2008, an essay by Rebecca Solnit inspired the term "mansplaining," which describes situations in which a man explains something to a woman who knows more about it than he does. "Manvising" hasn't made it into our lexicon yet, but most women find the phenomenon equally familiar. The term describes moments when men give women advice that they have neither asked for nor want. Solnit herself provided this very simple illustration in an article she wrote in 2022: "A few years ago, a friend of mine got married, and when I pulled up to the rustic wedding site, a man I didn't know positioned himself behind my car to make dramatic hand signals. I didn't need or ask for help, but he was giving it, and I'm sure he thought the credit for my success in parking my small car in this very easy spot was at least partly his."

Solnit's implication is that this man provided unsolicited advice because he thought that his skills were superior to hers since he was a man. That could have been his thinking, but research reveals that men are as likely to give unsolicited advice to other men as they are to women. Research also reveals that women give considerable amounts of advice to other women. It's with cross-gender feedback that the discrepancy becomes clear: One research project showed that men are five times as likely to give unrequested advice to women as women are to give it to men.

That's a problem because while providing advice can indeed be generous and kind, it also creates the impression that you're putting yourself above the person you're giving it to. In my own research I've interviewed dozens of men and women about this phenomenon. I've found that although most men don't believe they're guilty of manvising, well over 90% of women report that they have recently received unsolicited advice from their male colleagues.

One of my interviewees, a software industry marketing VP I'll call Cassandra, provided an example. At an all-hands meeting attended by 2,000 colleagues, she had to give two presentations about a major project she was leading. In the first she presented the results of nine months of work. She was anxious because the reception she got could make or break the project. Despite her fears, she felt she'd aced the presentation and, elated, made her way to the speakers' lounge to wait for the second presentation. There she bumped into her colleague Miles, who had spoken earlier that morning.

Here's what happened next: "I was pleased to relax and have a chat," Cassandra recalls. "After a few friendly exchanges, Miles surprised me with feedback: 'Your presentation was 90% perfect. The audience was eating it up! I do think you spoke a little too fast, which made you sound nervous. Also, maybe your mouth was too close to the mic because your voice somehow sounded tinny.' Although Miles's feedback in retrospect was actionable and meant to help before I went back onstage, I felt like he had hijacked my self-confidence. I had been feeling great about what I'd accomplished, and now I felt like an inexperienced child receiving coaching from a teacher. I noticed my body physically shifting back in my chair to get as far away from Miles as possible."

As Cassandra's story demonstrates, even when feedback is provided with a genuine desire to help, it clearly gives the person dispensing it emotional power over the person on the receiving end. One study has found that when people get spontaneous feedback, their heart rate jumps to a level that indicates moderate or extreme duress. It's no wonder that when one person offers feedback to another, the recipient's composure is shaken.

Research also shows that the act of providing advice makes people feel more powerful. One study asked 94 library employees how often they gave advice during their workday. The more advice someone gave, the more powerful that individual reported feeling. In another study the same researchers asked 188 students to read and respond to a written account of a student struggling to choose a major. Both the act of dispensing the advice and later being told that the student had read the advice increased the subjects' feeling of power.

All this makes cross-gender feedback tricky. A member of the majority (a male colleague, for example) who provides feedback to someone from an underrepresented group (like a woman in a management position) is likely to come off as belittling—even when sincerely trying to help.

History isn't destiny, however. Using what I call the "three A's of feedback," you can teach your workforce how to offer advice in a way that gets the useful input out there while still balancing the power dynamics. The first A is that feedback must be intended to *assist*. (It should always be provided with the genuine intention of helping your counterpart succeed and never be given just to get frustration off your chest.) The second is that it must be *actionable*. If it's not crystal clear from your input what your counterpart can do to improve, then keep it to yourself.

The third A is to *ask* for feedback before you provide it. This is especially important with cross-gender interactions. Unless someone has specifically requested your advice (in which case, jump in and give it), solicit suggestions about your own work before you offer anyone your insights. If Miles had started his discussion with Cassandra by saying, "I'd love to hear any thoughts you have about my presentation this morning," he would have put her in a position of power before turning the tables, which would have led her to treat his advice as valuable help rather than an attempt to assert dominance.

3. Feedback Across Generations: Create an Explicit Team Culture

Generational diversity in the workplace has increased significantly over the past decades, as people are living longer, healthier lives and retiring later. In today's organizations people might be collaborating with colleagues from four generations all at once—something unheard of a few decades ago.

I started to become interested in age diversity at work 25 years ago in my first management role. I had hired a woman who was exactly the same age as my mother to join my team. A pharmacist by training, Carole was elegant and worldly and was taking on her first job after spending 18 years raising children. I still remember how awkward I felt when she began having difficulty with a client and I had to give her corrective guidance. The age difference hadn't seemed a problem when things were going well, but I couldn't figure out how to avoid coming off as obnoxious when I outlined which behaviors she needed to change.

The experience I was having is sometimes referred to as *status incongruence.* This basically means that the status accorded your role in society doesn't match the part you're playing in the current context. One research project with 8,000 employees in Germany showed that when younger managers supervise older workers, status incongruence has a measurable negative impact on employees' happiness. It's not just that I feel strange treating my elder as my subordinate. As the researchers of this study concluded, the role reversal constantly suggests to the older subordinate that that person has somehow "failed to keep pace."

To complicate the challenge further, each succeeding generation has developed its own ideas about who should give feedback to whom, how formal or spontaneous that feedback should be, and how much praise versus criticism should be articulated. One member may expect that feedback will be given annually from boss to subordinate, for instance, and another that real-time feedback will be given in all directions. Here are a few of the key differences:

Baby Boomers (now in their late fifties and sixties and seventies) were the first to get graded in school on "works well with others." They were also the first to have work discussions about interpersonal effectiveness and emotional intelligence and saw feedback as a way to improve both. Though previous generations were more likely to hint at what should be done differently than to state feedback outright, Boomers introduced the annual performance review. According to the generational researcher Lynne Lancaster (coauthor of *When Generations Collide*), they learned that feedback should be formal and documented and given in annual meetings between boss and subordinate.

Gen Xers (in their forties to mid-fifties) grew up with rising divorce rates and two-income families. Left to fend for themselves at home, these "latchkey kids" learned to get along without an authority figure. Do-it-yourselfers, they relied on notes from Mom explaining how to cook pasta. They tend to be considerably less formal than their Boomer colleagues and don't want to wait all year to know how they're doing. They are the first generation to begin giving upward feedback to the boss. And according to Lancaster, they're more likely to want feedback instantaneously.

Millennials, or Generation Y (in their late twenties and thirties), were raised when child-rearing psychology focused on building self-esteem. A product of helicopter parenting and the philosophy that "every child gets a trophy," they're sometimes referred to sarcastically as the "snowflake generation" (because they're sensitive and easily crushed). But according to the generational expert Neil Howe (who coauthored *Generations*), this stereotype is misleading. Millennials do have high self-esteem, he says, but their self-confidence seems to be correlated with emotional resilience.

Research conducted in 2019 showed that when it comes to accepting feedback, Millennials are less sensitive than their older colleagues are. Though members of this generation expect and appreciate frequent and copious praise, don't expect them to wilt when the criticism is tough.

Zoomers (in their teens to mid-twenties) were the first generation to grow up surrounded by social media. With YouTube channels and TikTok platforms they came of age in a world of constant informal feedback. Zoomers learned to post something on social media in the morning and watch reactions come in all day long. They are more likely to expect to give and receive frequent, real-time feedback in all directions (subordinate to boss, peer to peer, and so on).

The cross-generational tensions these differences engender are captured nicely by the experience of Richard, a business writer in his late fifties who works in a major media group. Recently he attended a session where all the members of his department took turns giving one another feedback on their current projects. First a couple of other senior colleagues gave Richard both praise and tips for improving his work. Then it was Connor's turn.

A talented writer in his mid-twenties, Connor was less flattering. "This is all right," he told Richard, "but you completely left your personality out. Your audience wants to feel that you're with them, but your individual voice is absent." Richard took it badly. "Something about getting feedback from this kid who has decades less experience than me felt very uncomfortable," he recalls. "My immediate reaction was to reject his comments. I wasn't ready to listen to what he was saying, let alone collaborate with him again."

Not only was Connor decades younger than Richard, leading to status incongruence, but in Richard's Baby Boomer generation, feedback from someone who is not your boss is infrequent and inappropriate. Richard left the meeting shaking his head at this inexperienced kid telling him his writing was missing a clear voice.

If you're leading a multigenerational team, the best way to deal with diverse expectations about feedback is often to outline explicit norms for how and when it should be given. That creates a common platform on which all can converge.

Despite the discomfort Richard felt when receiving criticism from Connor, he understood that Connor was behaving in line with the culture of the team. This pushed him to stop and reflect. "After I got home, I started to think about the feedback I'd received," Richard says. "It became clear that Connor's had been the most valuable. The guys who come from my generation have a similar perspective to my own, but Connor's different perspective pushed me to see how to make my writing richer. He was right. My experience as a journalist had taught me to leave myself out of my writing, and in this case it made the piece feel sterile. The fact that Connor comes from a generation where people self-disclose more openly made it easier for him to pinpoint what my writing was lacking. I went back to it with new eyes and wrote something infinitely better."

4. Getting Everyone in the Feedback Loop

Most recent research has focused on the benefits of real-time feedback. See the problem, correct the problem. That's OK if you're the boss passing feedback on to your staff. But if you're younger and less experienced (or working on any highly diverse team), stopping colleagues in the hall to tell them how they could do their jobs better is likely to put your teammates on the defensive, make you a bunch of enemies, and maybe even stunt your career.

There is one mechanism that effectively surfaces all the diverse feedback learn-it-alls need to thrive. If you build regular loops for feedback into collaborations, your team will recognize it not as a sign of condescension or malevolence but as an integral part of the job. This involves setting aside specific moments for mutual exchanges: I know I'm expected to listen openly as you give me actionable feedback about what you think I've done well and what I could do to improve. Then I will do the same for you. Just like brushing our teeth, we do it regularly, to keep team performance high.

In setting up any loop, you need to clarify how much positive versus constructive feedback each teammate should supply. You can, for example, have people structure their feedback as one thing they feel that the other person is doing well and one thing the other person could do to up their performance. Alternatively, you can use a "start, stop, continue" structure, describing one thing to start doing, one thing to stop doing, and one thing to continue.

Given the maturity and cohesion of your team, you may institute loops that are more or less public. Here are three possible approaches:

One-to-one chats.

If your team members have never given one another feedback, a good initial step is to ask your immediate reports to meet individually with each of their team members in the coming month to share feedback, following the ground rules just described. The feedback remains between the two teammates.

"Speed-dating" sessions.

If team relationships are closer, you may be ready to share a little more openly. Ask participants to prepare rapid-fire feedback for one another. Send them off in pairs for six minutes of discussion, with each giving feedback for three minutes. Then have everyone move on to another colleague. At the end of the meeting, have all team members report back to the group on one helpful piece of feedback they received that they will act on.

Live 360-degree feedback circles.

If you have a mature team with strong relationships, get members together over a meal and take turns. If I'm up first, the person to my left gives me feedback (in front of the group). I listen and say thank you. Then the person to the left of that team member gives me feedback. Once we've completed the circle, we move on to the next recipient. At the end each person reports one key takeaway from the feedback received.

Exchanging feedback in front of a team requires courage but offers clear advantages. It stops members from whispering behind one another's backs and encourages the entire team to see feedback as a normal and healthy way to achieve success. One person who experienced a 360-degree circle told me, "Getting publicly ripped apart sounds like torture. Each time I go to a live 360, I'm nervous. But after you get started, you see it'll be fine. Because everyone is watching, people are careful to be generous and supportive with the single intention of helping you succeed. No one wants to embarrass or attack you. Everyone gets a lot of tough advice, so you're not singled out. When your turn comes, it might be difficult to hear what people have to say, but this is one of the greatest developmental gifts of your life."

Once you have the right feedback loops in place, you're on your way to building a team full of learn-it-alls who thrive on diverse perspectives. If your group is made up of people from a variety of cultures, genders, and generations, getting your employees to give feedback to one another frequently and openly allows each to get myriad ideas for how to improve, pushes the team toward excellence, exposes blind spots, and promotes greater cohesion. That's how you can make sure DEI and radical candor converge rather than collide.

Originally published in September–October 2023. Reprint R2305F

Want Stronger Relationships at Work? Change the Way You Listen

by Manbir Kaur

Roan walked into the office, listening to his favorite morning mix. As he neared his desk, his manager, Andy, intercepted him. Roan removed one earbud. "There's a problem with the report you submitted yesterday," Andy said. "I think it needs to be reworked. Could you get to it ASAP?"

"Was that really the first thing Andy could say to me this morning?" Roan thought.

With half his mind still on his music and the other half trying to adjust his plan for the morning, Roan shook his head without a word and walked on.

"Was he even listening?" Andy was a little offended.

A lot happens in the brain during conversations. The late Judith Glaser, author of *Conversational Intelligence*, writes that, in a conversation, our brain takes just 0.07 seconds to form an initial impression of the other person's intent—deciding whether or not we trust that person. Our actual response is then influenced by that impression. By that measure, Andy and Roan's conversation can only be deemed "poor."

Simplifying the Neurochemistry of Listening

In her book, Glaser quotes multiple researchers to explain that when we sense threat in a conversation, the amygdala (part of the limbic system in our brain) triggers the protection mode and a few hormones, such as cortisol, are released. When cortisol floods through our bodies, we may not be able to engage and connect, and we are likely to become more reactive, emotional, and impulsive. We also tend to perceive situations more negatively.

On the other hand, conversations that encourage cooperation and understanding result in the release of a different set of hormones, including oxytocin, which reinforce a bonding experience. That is when we stop being protective and begin to connect with others to build lasting relationships based on mutual trust.

By choosing the way we listen, we have the power to influence the neurochemical reactions that happen in the brain.

How We Listen

Glaser's framework on conversational intelligence suggests that we listen with three prominent attitudes. Each one influences how the speaker will respond to us.

Listening to protect.
You're on the defensive. You are trying to protect your identity and your space. The speaker may feel ignored.

Listening to accept or reject.
You are listening with an intent to judge. The speaker may feel labeled. You'll often see examples of this during a team meeting.

Idea in Brief

The Challenge

The way we listen to others may play a major role in building stronger relationships at work. Research shows that in a conversation it takes the brain just 0.07 seconds to form an initial impression of the other person's intent—to decide whether to trust that person or not. When we sense threat in a conversation, stress hormones are released and we may not be able to engage and connect.

The Path Forward

To become a better listener, four approaches can help: Go in with the right intention. Use both your head and heart. Put yourself in the other person's shoes. And show that you're engaged.

Listening to co-create.

You are listening to connect with the other person, and there is psychological safety. You begin with the intent to explore and understand:

- What are they trying to say?

- What are they thinking?

- What are they expecting to explore with me?

- How can I connect to their world?

When you chose to listen with openness, the neurochemistry of both your own body and that of the other person will come to your aid, creating the opportunity to build greater understanding.

In fact, listening is fun and can give you fresh new perspectives.

How to Be a Good Listener

To develop better listening habits, practice these four tips in your next conversation:

Join with the right intention.
When you are in a conversation, begin with an intention to really listen to the other person. Make sure that you believe they have something of value to say and that it is important for you to give them a chance to say it.

If Roan had immediately removed both earbuds, Andy wouldn't have felt ignored.

Instead of blaming Roan for the problem in the report, Andy could have set the context and asked if any of his instructions had been unclear, perhaps leading to the problems in the report.

Use both your head and your heart.
Try to understand not just the "what" but also the "why." Good listening will help you both understand the reasons and connect with the emotions behind what's being said.

Roan could have acknowledged the mistake. "I'm sorry that the report didn't meet your expectations. Please help me understand how I can make improvements." Expressing and acknowledging those feelings clearly could set the stage for a stronger conversation and also help build trust between them.

Andy could have been more sensitive, instead of ambushing Roan just as he walked in. "I am sorry for catching you now, as I see you're just getting into work, but this is really urgent. Do you have a minute?"

Put yourself in the other person's shoes.
No one understands your situation and challenges, right? Well, that perspective applies for the other person too. So listen with empathy and compassion. Even if your own constraints prevent you from helping them, at least you can listen thoughtfully.

Roan could have acknowledged the urgency behind Andy's request and reassured him that he would get to it as soon as possible. He could have said, "Of course I understand the client needs the report urgently. I'll see what I can do to improve it right away."

Andy could have spent a moment trying to explain the specifics of what was wrong with the report. Perhaps Roan needed clearer instructions. "I know you worked hard on the report, but it's not what the client wants. Maybe my instructions weren't clear. Can I help you with additional information?"

Show that you're engaged.

Give the conversation your full attention. Ask open-ended questions to understand things better.

Roan should have asked how he could make the report better. A question like "I may need help. Could you give me more information so I can make the report stronger? What did the client not like about the report?" serves the purpose.

Try these tips for the next few conversations you have, and see how you develop personal relationships with deeper connections. The more actively you listen, the more you will be heard.

Reprinted from hbr.org, originally published July 17, 2020.

How to Navigate Conflict with a Coworker

by Amy Gallo

EARLY IN MY CAREER I took a job reporting to someone who had a reputation for being difficult. I'll call her Elise. Plenty of people warned me that she would be hard to work with, but I thought I could handle it. I prided myself on being able to get along with anyone. I didn't let people get under my skin. I could see the best in everyone.

Two months later I was ready to quit.

Elise worked long days and on weekends and expected her team to do the same. Her assumptions about what could get done in a day were wildly unreasonable. She often followed up at 8:30 a.m. on a request she'd made at 6:00 the night before. She disparaged my teammates in front of me, questioning their work ethic and commitment to the company. She would scroll through colleagues' calendars and point out how little they'd accomplished despite having a meeting-free day.

I vowed to stop caring so much about how she acted and to treat her with kindness. In a good week I could succeed. But more often than not those lofty intentions flew out the window. The minute she insinuated that I wasn't working hard enough, I would clench my teeth, roll my eyes behind her back, and complain about her to my coworkers.

Interpersonal conflicts like that—with insecure bosses, know-it-all colleagues, passive-aggressive peers—are common at work, and it's easy to get caught up in them. In one study 94% of respondents said they had worked with a "toxic" person in the previous five years. Another survey—of 2,000 U.S. workers—indicated that their top source of tension on the job was relationships. Trapped in these negative dynamics, we find it hard to be our best selves or to improve the situation. Instead we spend time worrying, react in regrettable ways that violate our values, avoid difficult colleagues, and sometimes even withdraw from work entirely. But those responses can lead to a host of bad outcomes, including reduced creativity, slower and worse decision-making, and even fatal mistakes. For example, as Christine Porath wrote for the *New York Times,* in "a survey of more than 4,500 doctors, nurses and other hospital personnel, 71 percent tied disruptive behavior, such as abusive, condescending or insulting personal conduct, to medical errors, and 27 percent tied such behavior to patient deaths."

None of us is perfect when it comes to navigating the complexity of human relationships. Especially in times of stress, or when we feel threatened, even the most seasoned workplace veterans can find themselves focusing on the short-term goal of ego or reputation protection (*I need to win this argument or to look good in front of my team*) rather than the long-term one of behaving honorably and preserving collegiality.

So how can we return to our best selves? Having studied conflict management and resolution over the past several years, I've outlined seven strategies that will help you work more effectively with difficult colleagues. These aren't silver bullets that will magically transform your problem coworker into your best friend, but they should make your interactions more tolerable if not more positive. And they'll help you build interpersonal resilience so that you feel less stressed when you're engaged in a conflict and can bounce back from it more quickly.

Idea in Brief

The Challenge

Interpersonal conflicts are common in the workplace, and it's easy to get caught up in them. But that can lead to reduced creativity, slower and worse decision-making, and even fatal mistakes. So how can we return to our best selves?

The Path Forward

Seven principles can help you work more effectively with difficult colleagues: (1) Understand that your perspective is not the only one possible. (2) Be aware of and question any unconscious biases you may be harboring. (3) View the conflict not as me-versus-them but as a problem to be jointly solved. (4) Understand what outcome you're aiming for. (5) Be very judicious in discussing the issue with others. (6) Experiment with behavior change to find out what will improve the situation. (7) Stay curious about the other person and explore how you can more effectively work together.

1. Remember that Your Perspective Is Just One Among Many

We all come to the workplace with different viewpoints and values. We might disagree on everything from whether it's OK to be five minutes late to a meeting to acceptable ways of interrupting a colleague to the appropriate consequences for someone who's made a mistake. It's not realistic to expect your boss, teammates, or reports to see eye to eye with you all the time.

When such differences of opinion arise, however, most of us believe that we're seeing the issue objectively and correctly, and anyone who has another view is uninformed, irrational, or biased. Social psychologists refer to that tendency as *naive realism*. For example, in one study, participants who were asked to tap out the rhythm of a well-known song, such as "Happy Birthday," predicted that listeners would be able to name the tune about 50% of the time. They were sure that it would be clear to others what they were trying to convey. But the guesses were accurate only 2.5% of the time! Once we're confident about something—whether it's our ability to tap out a song or the solution to this quarter's budget shortfall—we find it hard to imagine that others won't see it the same way.

It's important to recognize and resist this gut reaction. Challenge your own perspective by asking questions such as: How do I know that what I believe is true? What if I'm wrong? How would I change my behavior? What assumptions have I made? How would someone with different values and experiences see things? The answers to those questions matter less than the exercise of asking them. They are a good way of reminding yourself that your view is just that: *your view.* Not everyone sees things the same way—and that's OK.

Indeed, you and your colleagues don't need to reach consensus on "the facts" of what's happened or who's to blame for a problem. Instead of spending hours debating whose interpretation is correct, shift your focus to what should happen going forward.

2. Be Aware of Your Biases

Biases creep into all sorts of workplace interactions. One common derailer of colleagues' relationships is *fundamental attribution error*—an inclination to assume that other people's behavior has more to do with their personality than with the situation, while believing the opposite of oneself. For example, you might presume that a teammate who's late to a meeting is disorganized or disrespectful rather than caught in traffic or stuck in another meeting that went long. But when *you're* running behind, you might focus on the circumstances that led to your tardiness.

A related cognitive shortcut that creates problems is *confirmation bias,* or the tendency to interpret events or evidence as proving the truth of existing beliefs. If your view of your colleague Andrew is already negative, you're more likely to interpret his actions as further evidence that he's not up to the task, he's unkind, or he cares only about himself—and it will be increasingly difficult for him to prove you wrong.

Even what we consider difficult behavior can be shaped by the prejudices we carry into the workplace. Earlier in my career I worked with a client—a Black woman—whose ideas I hesitated to challenge, even though that was part of my job as a consultant. I was afraid I'd get a strong reaction, despite the fact that she had never so much as raised her voice in previous encounters. I had fallen into believing the "angry Black woman" stereotype. Now I know to watch out for *affinity bias,* an unconscious tendency to align with people who are similar to us in appearance, beliefs, and background. Research shows that when colleagues aren't like us—in terms of gender, race, ethnicity, education, physical abilities, or position at work—we are less comfortable around them and thus less likely to want to work with them.

How can you interrupt those biases? First, get a better sense of your susceptibility to them by taking an online quiz such as the one from Project Implicit, a nonprofit started by researchers at Harvard, the University of Washington, and the University of Virginia. When you're struggling with a coworker, ask yourself, What role could my biases be playing here? Is it possible I'm not seeing the situation clearly because I'm making assumptions about this person, or unwilling to rethink my initial impression, or unconsciously focusing on our differences?

Play devil's advocate and question your own interpretation of the situation. I learned the "flip it to test it" approach from a TEDx talk by Kristen Pressner, the global head of human resources at a multinational firm: If your colleague was a different gender, race, or sexual orientation or had a different place in the hierarchy, would you make the same assumptions? Would you say the same things or treat that person the same way?

Finally, ask someone you trust—and who will tell you the truth—to help you reflect on the ways in which you might be seeing the situation unfairly.

3. Don't Make It "Me Against Them"

In a disagreement it's easy to think in polarizing ways: "me versus you," enemies at war. One person is being difficult; the other isn't. One person is right; the other is wrong.

To break out of that mental model, instead imagine that there are not two but three entities in the situation: you, your colleague, and the dynamic between you. Maybe that third entity is something specific: a decision you must make together or an assignment you need to complete. Or maybe it's more general: ongoing tension or rivalry between you or bad blood over a project gone wrong. Rather than work to change your colleague, try to make progress on that third thing.

Take Andre, who was struggling with his colleague Emilia. Whenever he proposed a new idea, she produced a list of reasons why it would never work. For a long time Andre saw the two of them as opponents. When I asked how he pictured their dynamic, he told me he saw a dark cloud over her head and a bright sun over his. But that visualization reinforced his view of the situation, prompting him to brace for battle every time he spoke with her. Eventually he decided to shift to less-antagonistic thinking. He started to picture the conflict between them as a seesaw. Though they sat on opposite ends, they could perhaps work together to find balance. That helped him view her as a collaborator rather than an adversary.

No one wants to have a nemesis at work. So think of problematic coworkers as colleagues with whom you share a problem to be solved.

4. Know Your Goal

To avoid drama and stay focused on the work, you need to be clear about your goals. Do you want to get a project over the finish line? Build a healthy working relationship that will last into the future? Feel less angry or frustrated after your interactions?

Make a list of your goals (big and small) and then circle the most important ones. Your intentions will determine—consciously and subconsciously—how you act. For instance, if your goal is to avoid getting stuck in long discussions with a pessimistic colleague, you'll need to take actions different from those you'd take if your goal was to keep the person's naysaying from bringing down the team.

It's fine to set your sights low. Often it's enough to focus on just having a functional relationship—getting to a point where your skin doesn't crawl when Ethan's name shows up in your inbox or you're not losing sleep at night because Marjorie is making your life miserable. Multiple and more-ambitious goals are OK too. For example, if you're arguing with your insecure boss about which metrics to report to the senior leadership team, your goals might be to: (1) come up with stats that you can both live with, (2) make sure the senior team knows about your expertise, and (3) find a way to avoid heated disagreements before big meetings in the future.

Once you've decided what you want to accomplish, write it down on a piece of paper. Research has shown that people who vividly describe or picture their goals are 1.2 to 1.4 times as likely to achieve them, and that objectives recorded by hand are more likely to be realized. Refer to your goals before interacting with your colleague to keep your eyes on the prize.

5. Avoid Workplace Venting and Gossip—Mostly

It's natural to turn to others when something is off at work. You might want to confirm that you're not misinterpreting a vague email, get advice on advancing a stalled initiative, or simply be reassured that you're a good person. And if your colleague says, "Yes, Greta does seem grumpy. What's up with that?" you get a little jolt of relief: *It's not just me.*

That type of side conversation, whether it happens digitally or in person, can be considered venting. But you might also call it gossip. Despite its bad rap, research shows gossip can play an important role in bonding with coworkers. When you learn that Marina in marketing also finds Michael in finance difficult and knows of others who feel the same, it fosters a sense of connection. You've essentially formed an in-group that has information that others, especially Michael, don't. And Marina's validation of your perspective gives you a rush of feel-good adrenaline and dopamine.

Studies have also shown that gossip can be beneficial in deterring people from behaving selfishly. If difficult colleagues realize that others are speaking badly of them and warning teammates about working with them, they're more likely to change their ways.

Of course, there are also dangers to venting and gossiping. First, they heighten the risk of confirmation bias. Sure, Michael may be exasperating sometimes, but once you and your work friends start talking about it, you're more likely to interpret his future actions in a negative light. Occasional missteps are painted as an inherent trait, and the "Michael is difficult" storyline becomes entrenched. Second, gossiping often reflects poorly on the gossiper. Although you may get the immediate validation you're seeking, you may also get a reputation for being unprofessional—or end up labeled as the difficult one.

It is perfectly legitimate to seek help with sorting out your feelings or to check with someone else that you're seeing things clearly. But choose whom you talk to (and what you share) carefully. Look for people who are constructive, have your best interests at heart, will challenge your perspective when they disagree, and can be discreet.

6. Experiment to Find What Works

There isn't one right way to get a know-it-all to stop being condescending or your passive-aggressive colleague to deal with you in a more straightforward way. The strategies you choose will depend on the context: who you are, who the other person is, the nature of your relationship, the norms and culture of your workplace, and so on.

Start by coming up with two or three methods you want to test out. Often small actions can have a big impact. Then design an experiment: Determine what you'll do differently, pick a period of time to try it out, and see how it works. For example, if you want to improve communication with a difficult colleague, you might decide that for two weeks you're going to ignore that person's tone and focus on the underlying message. Don't assume the tactic will fix everything wrong between you; view it as an experiment that will teach you something, even if it's only that the approach doesn't work.

Keep trying, tweaking, and refreshing experiments or abandoning ones that don't produce results. For example, if you've tried to handle a colleague's lack of follow-through by sending post-meeting emails that confirm what everyone has agreed to do, but the person still fails to keep promises, then don't keep sending the emails expecting different results. Try something else. As the conflict expert Jennifer Goldman-Wetzler explains, you'll need to find another way to "interrupt the conflict pattern of the past"—often by doing something the other person doesn't expect.

7. Be—and Stay—Curious

Salvador Minuchin, an Argentine therapist, wrote, "Certainty is the enemy of change." When dealing with a negative coworker, it's easy to think, *It's always going to be this way* or *That person will never change.* But resignation and pessimism will get you nowhere. Instead, adopt a curious mindset and maintain hope that your troubled relationship can be improved.

Research shows that curiosity brings a host of benefits: It wards off confirmation bias, prevents stereotyping, and helps us approach tough situations not with aggression (fight) or defensiveness (flight) but with creativity. The key is to shift from drawing often unflattering conclusions to posing genuine questions. When your colleague Jada starts complaining that she's doing more work than anyone else on the team, don't think, *Here we go again with Jada's attitude.* Instead ask yourself, What's going on with her? This feels familiar, but what have I missed in the past? Why is she acting like this?

Try to catch yourself in unproductive thought patterns; then step back and take stock, Who gets along well with Jada, and how do they interact with each other? Have there been times when Jada was more pleasant and cooperative? What was different about those situations?

When you hit a rough patch with someone, think about instances at work or elsewhere when you and another person didn't get along at first but were able to get past it, and reflect on those experiences with curiosity. How were you able to persevere? What helped you achieve resolution? Finally, consider exactly what you stand to gain from meeting the goals you've set out to achieve in a work relationship. Project into the future. If you overcome the conflict, what will be different? How will your work life improve?

You can't be certain of what the future holds for you and your colleague, so be curious instead. It may snap you out of a mindset that's keeping you from discovering an unexpected solution to your problem.

———————————

No matter what type of difficult colleague you're dealing with or what you decide to do next, these seven strategies can improve your odds of responding productively, establishing appropriate boundaries, and building stronger, more fulfilling collaborations at work. Sometimes change isn't possible, in which case you'll eventually need to cut your losses in a relationship and focus on protecting your career and well-being. But I've found that with good-faith efforts and hard work, even some of the trickiest interpersonal conflicts can be resolved.

Originally published in September–October 2022. Reprint R2205L

Coaching for Change

by Richard Boyatzis, Melvin Smith, and Ellen Van Oosten

CHANGE IS HARD. Ask anyone who has tried to switch careers, develop a new skill, improve a relationship, or break a bad habit. And yet for most people change will at some point be necessary— a critical step toward fulfilling their potential and achieving their goals, both at work and at home. They will need support with this process. They'll need a coach.

That's where you come in. Whether you're a boss or a colleague, a friend or a spouse, introverted or extroverted, emotional or analytic, or high or low on the totem pole, you can learn how to facilitate life-enhancing change in those around you.

All three of us work as professional coaches to executives in a variety of career stages, functions, industries, and countries. We've also spent the past two decades investigating how coaching works and training others to do it. We've conducted dozens of longitudinal studies and field experiments to identify evidence-based strategies, and we're sharing them here to ensure that more people are equipped to help others become their best selves.

In 1970 one of us (Richard) developed a theory of intentional change, which has become canon in psychology and management science. Intentional change involves envisioning the ideal self (who you wish to *be* and what you want to *do* in your work and life); exploring the real self (the gaps you need to fill and the strengths that will help you do so); developing a learning agenda (a road map for turning aspirations into reality); and then experimenting and practicing (with new behaviors and roles).

Good coaches help people through this process. Note that we used the word "help," not "guide," "lead," "push," or "pull." You're not there to tell anyone what to do. You're there to ask good questions and listen intently, to offer compassion, to explore a person's individual vision, and to build a caring relationship. Your job is to assist someone else with making a change, and how you go about it matters. You're there to help them spot the learning opportunity, set the groundwork, and see things through. This framework will let you support people with challenges that range from very big (I'm unsatisfied in my career) to relatively small (I'd like to interact with others differently). Here's how it works.

Spot the Opportunity

If you pay attention, you'll start finding what we call "coachable moments"—opportunities to help people with their development—everywhere. Sometimes people are aware they need to shift gears: The challenge is evident. They get a promotion, are tapped to lead a significant project, or receive some feedback that their approach needs to be retooled. In other cases they experience a wake-up call: They lose their job in the latest downsizing, get a scary health diagnosis, or hit a major birthday milestone. But often they may have only a vague sense or no idea at all that things aren't quite right in their lives.

Let's look at the experiences of two executives. The first, Karen Milley, was the head of R&D at a large consumer goods company and oversaw 60 engineers and scientists. As a leader, she was driven and direct. Her focus was on solving immediate problems, and she got results. But when her manager asked her to enroll in a corporate leadership-development program, she began to wonder if her transactional, no-nonsense style was really helping her get the best performance out of her team.

The second executive, Ray Lewis, was a corporate accounts manager at his family's business, an environmental emergency response

Idea in Brief

The Potential

Whether you're a boss, a colleague, or a friend, you can help the people around you make important life-enhancing changes. But the way to do that isn't by setting targets for them and fixing their problems; it's by coaching with compassion, an approach that involves focusing on their dreams and how they could achieve them.

The Path Forward

Instead of doling out advice, a good coach will ask exploratory, open-ended questions and listen with genuine care and concern. The idea is to have coachees envision an ideal self (whom they wish to be and what they wish to do), explore the real self (not just the gaps they need to fill but the strengths that will help them do so), set a learning agenda, and then experiment with and practice new behaviors and roles. The coach is there to provide support as people strive to spot their learning opportunities, set the groundwork to achieve change, and then see things through.

service, and on track to succeed his father as president. He'd even enrolled in an executive MBA course to hone his leadership skills. But he was feeling increasingly uneasy.

In both cases, the learning opportunity was clear. Milley was a standout manager who hoped to reach the C-suite, but she hadn't yet developed an inspiring leadership style. Lewis had never truly thought about or decided on his ideal career path. He'd just followed the one laid out for him, and if you asked him about taking over from his dad, his lack of genuine excitement came through. He needed to discover passion for his work.

Critically, Milley and Lewis were also ready to grow. Both were finally willing to look at an important aspect of their lives in new or different ways. When you're considering whether to invest in coaching someone, you need to ask yourself: Is this individual open to change? Are they willing to engage in the reflection and experimentation necessary to make it happen? Research by Bruce Avolio of the University of Washington's Foster School of Business and Sean Hannah of Wake Forest University shows that it's useful for companies to assess and sometimes enhance the readiness of employees they've chosen for leadership development; otherwise, it won't be as effective.

Set the Groundwork

Numerous studies have shown that people tend to achieve more, in a more sustainable way, when they're in a positive state both psychologically and physically. How can you get someone into the right mindset? By coaching with compassion. You start by showing genuine care and concern for the other person so that the two of you can build what we call a "resonant relationship." You also need to display curiosity—asking exploratory, open-ended questions designed to help the person realize their personal vision, which becomes the context for your work together.

Unfortunately, when faced with a coachable moment, most of us tend to do the opposite. We drill down into the problem and then offer advice and solutions. As an engineer-turned-marketing-executive we know once said, "When people come to me with a problem, I see the problem, not the person. Actually, I see people as problem-bearing platforms!" This is coaching for compliance, and it can be effective in helping someone achieve a specific predetermined goal, such as earning a promotion. But when it comes to broader behavioral goals, such as becoming a dynamic leader or a great listener or finding a better work/life balance, this strategy is less successful. Indeed, as our studies and other research have shown, it can trigger a stress response that hinders rather than helps progress.

In work with our Case Western Reserve University colleague Anthony Jack, for example, we found that students who were coached for compliance—with an emphasis on targets and on challenges they needed to overcome—were left feeling "guilty and self-conscious." Coaching that instead focused on personal dreams and how people might achieve them, in contrast, elicited positive emotions and was deemed by study subjects to be "inspiring and caring." What's more, our neuroimaging studies showed that it helped activate areas of their brains associated with openness to new ideas, change, and learning.

Compassionate coaching continues with the discovery of the ideal self—getting the person you're helping to tell you about their values, passions, identity, and hopes for the future. This requires you to set aside your own biases, assumptions, and experience, and engage in what MIT professor Ed Schein called "humble inquiry." You must demonstrate sincere interest in the person, convey empathy for their situation, communicate your deep desire to help, and then let them do at least 80% of the talking.

For example, you might ask Milley: Who are you at your very best? What kind of leader do you want to be? How do you want others in the organization to see you? What does success look like to you? What position do you ultimately want to attain? You might ask Lewis: What kind of work do you feel drawn to do? What gives you the greatest energy and excitement as you think about your future? What do you really want to do, and how does that differ from what you feel you should do? Twenty years from now, what would you like to say you've accomplished? (And the best last question is always: What other ideas come to mind as you think about this?)

Angela Passarelli, a professor at the College of Charleston, has compared the outcomes of a coaching experience centered on this vision of a positive future with those of coaching that instead focused on career advancement and encouraged people to work through their current problems. She discovered that participants who experienced the first kind of coaching felt happier, expressed higher aspirations, were willing to exert significantly more effort in pursuing their goals, and found more joy in doing so.

We advise everyone we coach to cap off the ideal-self discussions we've had—typically they involve multiple conversations—by crafting a personal vision statement. (Dewitt Jones, a prominent corporate trainer, goes so far as to ask that it be boiled down into a short phrase of six or so words and then memorized and repeated as a daily mantra.) This practice keeps people focused on their desire to change, rather than their obligation to. Milley's personal vision statement was "Live freely, in good health, with integrity, in a future filled with love and hope." Lewis's was "Enjoy the freedom to travel the world, meet interesting people, and pursue an exciting, passion-filled life of learning."

Next, you want to guide the person you're coaching toward an accurate assessment of their real self. This is not just about listing strengths and weaknesses. And it certainly doesn't involve highlighting places where the person needs improvement. Babson professor Scott Taylor, who has studied self-awareness for decades, suggests that it has two components: what people know about themselves, and their understanding of how others experience and think of them. The point here is to identify the areas where your coachee's perceptions differ from those of others and, even more critically, where their ideal self and real self are aligned or not.

Formal or informal 360-degree feedback can be useful here. So can additional nonleading, nonjudgmental questions, especially ones that focus on the person's best qualities and how they can be leveraged. Even when discussing areas for development, it's important to keep those being coached in that positive emotional state. As Andrew Carnegie reportedly once said, "Men are developed the same way that gold is mined. When gold is mined, several tons of dirt must be moved to get an ounce of gold, but one doesn't go into the mine looking for dirt—one goes in looking for gold."

We recommend capturing this work in a "personal balance sheet." In devising it people should consider not only their current strengths and weaknesses but also their most distinctive qualities and enduring characteristics—their traits, habits, and competencies that have held steady over time. This enables them to clarify both what is going well and what might need to change relative to their long-term vision. Milley recognized that while she excelled at maintaining her composure in difficult times and reading power dynamics throughout the organization, she wasn't adequately demonstrating the care and empathy for others that she genuinely felt. Lewis realized that his strong suit was being a visionary and adapting easily to diverse environments—and that he didn't want to continue subordinating his own dreams to perceived obligations and the expectations of others.

Next comes the learning agenda. How, exactly, will the individual you're coaching move from point A to point B? Again, we advocate for a focus on existing strengths, passions, and values. Ask how the knowledge, skills, and traits the person already possesses can be used to close any relevant gaps, and what behavioral change they are most excited to try.

The learning agenda is not a performance improvement plan designed to address shortcomings; those feel like work and inhibit the development process. The idea is to leave people feeling energized and empowered to improve. Milley decided that she wanted to be more of a coach and less of a commander and become more emotionally aware and mindful of others. Lewis's priorities included more fully integrating his personal passions with his professional goals, developing stronger relationships with key people within and outside the business, and making time to reflect on what was most important to him in life. That included activities like hiking, martial arts, and other sports; work with youth groups; meals and get-togethers with friends, family, and coworkers; and occasional extended breaks away from home and the office.

See Things Through

Change efforts of any kind require time and energy. Even the best-laid plans sometimes fail or take a while to pan out. Research by Phillippa Lally and her colleagues at University College London found that it takes 18 to 254 days to form a new habit. Skill building, relationship management, and career change require even greater commitments, with many stops and starts.

So a big part of a coach's job is to keep people progressing in the right direction—experimenting with new behaviors, testing different tactics, and then practicing and perfecting those that prove most effective.

Focused on her learning goals, Milley met regularly with her coach to review progress. She worked to shift out of her always-busy problem-solver mode and into being more approachable, kind, and playful with her team. She committed to spending more time with her direct reports in an effort to better understand their experiences and soon established more-authentic relationships.

Lewis and his coach also continued to check in periodically to review his progress and discuss certain unreconciled issues. But it took an extended vacation abroad—that is, the time for deep reflection Lewis had deeply desired—for things to finally click. Not long after it, he left the family business and started his own successful company.

The business of learning, growth, and changing one's identity and habits is not a solo act. It's so challenging that the people you coach will need continued support not only from you but also from an extended circle of others. Kathy Kram, a professor emeritus at Boston University's Questrom School of Business, and Monica Higgins of Harvard University's Graduate School of Education call this circle "a developmental network." We recommend that coachees create a personal board of advisers made up of role models for the types of behaviors they aspire to. The idea is to identify a group of people who have a stake in an individual's ultimate success and can serve as sources of inspiration and sometimes even accountability.

If you're a team leader, peer coaching is another powerful option. If you train others in the intentional change framework, they can serve as compassionate catalysts, seeing their colleagues through the transformation they've started and perhaps even helping them identify and embark on the next one. We've found that one-on-one peer relationships work well, but so do small groups of five to 12 peers.

When Carlos De Barnola, then the director of HR for the Iberian division of Covidien, brought peer coaching to his company, he asked each person to pair up with one teammate and talk, with one of the three of us in the room to help facilitate the conversation. Very quickly, people began to show more concern, ask good questions, and build real, trusting relationships. After a while, Barnola told these pairs to find another pair. They formed quartets, and soon we, the professionals, were able to withdraw entirely while the coaching continued.

If you're a manager, your most important job is to help those around you reach their greatest potential. Having been coached themselves, Karen Milley and Ray Lewis now bring what they've learned to their teams. "Today I give people permission to have two or three scenarios of a possible future, and I assure them that we'll figure out the path that's best for them," Milley says. "I'm seeing that compassion with each other leads to compassion with customers, constituents, and all others, which creates performance."

We agree: When you coach with compassion, it becomes contagious.

Originally published in September–October 2019. Reprint R1905L

The Science of Strong Business Writing

by Bill Birchard

STRONG WRITING SKILLS are essential for anyone in business. You need them to effectively communicate with colleagues, employees, and bosses and to sell any ideas, products, or services you're offering.

Many people, especially in the corporate world, think good writing is an art—and that those who do it well have an innate talent they've nurtured through experience, intuition, and a habit of reading often and widely. But every day we're learning more about the science of good writing. Advances in neurobiology and psychology show, with data and in images, exactly how the brain responds to words, phrases, and stories. And the criteria for making better writing choices are more objective than you might think.

Good writing gets the reader's dopamine flowing in the area of the brain known as the reward circuit. Great writing releases opioids that turn on reward hot spots. Just like good food, a soothing bath, or an enveloping hug, well-executed prose makes us feel pleasure, which makes us want to keep reading.

Most of the rules you learned in school—"Show, don't tell" or "Use the active voice"—still hold. But the reasons they do are now clearer. Scientists using MRI and PET machines can literally see how reward regions clustered in the midbrain light up when people read certain types of writing or hear it spoken aloud. Each word, phrase, or idea acts as a stimulus, causing the brain to instantly answer a stream of questions: Does this promise value? Will I like it? Can I learn from it?

Kent Berridge, a pioneering University of Michigan psychologist and neuroscientist, notes that researchers originally believed that the reward circuit largely handled sensory cues. But, he explains, "it's become clear in the past 50 years from neuroimaging studies that all kinds of social and cultural rewards can also activate this system."

Whether it's a succinct declarative statement in an email or a complex argument in a report, your own writing has the potential to light up the neural circuitry of your readers' brains. (The same is true if you read the words to an audience.) The magic happens when prose has one or more of these characteristics: It's simple, specific, surprising, stirring, seductive, smart, social, or story-driven. In my work as an author and a writing coach for businesspeople, I've found those eight S's to be hallmarks of the best writing. And scientific evidence backs up their power.

Simplicity

"Keep it simple." This classic piece of writing advice stands on the most basic neuroscience research. Simplicity increases what scientists call the brain's "processing fluency." Short sentences, familiar words, and clean syntax ensure that the reader doesn't have to exert too much brainpower to understand your meaning.

By contrast, studies have shown that sentences with clauses nested in the middle take longer to read and cause more comprehension mistakes. Ditto for most sentences in the passive voice. If you write "Profits are loved by investors," for example, instead of "Investors love profits," you're switching the standard positions of the verb and the direct object. That can cut comprehension accuracy by 10% and take a tenth of a second longer to read.

Idea in Brief

The Research

Brain scans are showing us in new detail exactly what entices readers. Scientists can see a group of midbrain neurons—the "reward circuit"—light up as people respond to everything from a simple metaphor to an unexpected story twist. The big takeaway? Whether you're crafting an email to a colleague or an important report for the board, you can write in a way that delights readers on a primal level, releasing pleasure chemicals in their brains.

How to Do It

There are eight features of satisfying writing: simplicity, specificity, surprise, stirring language, seductiveness, smart ideas, social content, and storytelling. They're effective tools for engaging readers because they trigger the same neural responses that other pleasurable stimuli do. Learning how to use these eight S's can captivate readers and help your message stick.

Tsuyoshi Okuhara, of the University of Tokyo, teamed with colleagues to ask 400 people aged 40 to 69 to read about how to exercise for better health. Half the group got long-winded, somewhat technical material. The other half got an easy-to-read edit of the same content. The group reading the simple version—with shorter words and sentences, among other things—scored higher on self-efficacy: They expressed more confidence in succeeding.

Even more noteworthy: Humans learn from experience that simpler explanations are not always right, but they *usually* are. Andrey Kolmogorov, a Russian mathematician, proved decades ago that people infer that simpler patterns yield better predictions, explanations, and decisions. That means you're more persuasive when you reduce overdressed ideas to their naked state.

Cutting extraneous words and using the active voice are two ways to keep it simple. Another tactic is to drill down to what's really salient and scrap tangential details. Let's say you have researched crossover markets and are recommending options in a memo to senior leaders. Instead of sharing every pro and con for each market—that is, taking the exhaustive approach—maybe pitch just the top two prospects and identify their principal pluses and minuses.

Specificity

Specifics awaken a swath of brain circuits. Think of "pelican" versus "bird." Or "wipe" versus "clean." In one study, the more-specific words in those pairs activated more neurons in the visual and motorstrip parts of the brain than did the general ones, which means they caused the brain to process meaning more robustly.

Years ago scientists thought our brains decoded words as symbols. Now we understand that our neurons actually "embody" what the words mean: When we hear more-specific ones, we "taste," "feel," and "see" traces of the real thing.

Remarkably, the simulation may extend to our muscles too. When a team led by an Italian researcher, Marco Tettamanti, asked people to listen to sentences related to the mouth, hand, and leg—"I bite an apple"; "I grasp a knife"; "I kick the ball"—the brain regions for moving their jaws, hands, and legs fired.

Using more-vivid, palpable language will reward your readers. In a recent letter to shareholders, Amazon CEO Jeff Bezos didn't say, "We're facing strong competition." Channeling Tettamanti's research, he wrote, "Third-party sellers are kicking our first-party butt. Badly."

Another specificity tactic is to give readers a memorable shorthand phrase to help them retain your message. Malcolm Gladwell coined "the tipping point." Management gurus W. Chan Kim and Renée Mauborgne came up with "blue ocean strategy"; essayist Nassim Nicholas Taleb, "black swan event."

Surprise

Our brains are wired to make nonstop predictions, including guessing the next word in every line of text. If your writing confirms the readers' guess, that's OK, though possibly a yawner. Surprise can make your message stick, helping readers learn and retain information.

Jean-Louis Dessalles, a researcher in artificial intelligence and cognitive science at Télécom Paris, conducted an experiment that demonstrated people's affinity for the unexpected. He asked participants to read short, unfinished narratives and consider different possible endings for each. For example, one story read: "Two weeks after my car had been stolen, the police informed me that a car that might be mine was for sale on the internet . . . . The phone number had been identified. It was the mobile phone number of . . . ." The choices were (a) "my office colleague," (b) "a colleague of my brother's," or (c) "someone in my neighborhood." For 17 of 18 stories, the vast majority of people preferred the most unexpected ending (in this example, the work colleague). They didn't want a story that fulfilled their predictions.

So reward your readers with novelty. Jonah Berger and Katherine Milkman, of the Wharton School, saw the impact of surprising content when they examined nearly 7,000 articles that appeared online in the *New York Times*. They found that those rated as surprising were 14% more likely to be on the newspaper's "most-emailed" list.

Readers appreciate unusual wordplay, too. A good example is John McPhee's characterization of World War II as a "technological piñata." Or consider how a Texas-based conglomerate described itself in its 2016 shareholder letter: "Think of Biglari Holdings as a museum of businesses. Our preference is to collect masterpieces."

Stirring Language

You may think you're more likely to persuade with logic, but no. Our brains process the emotional connotations of a word within 200 milliseconds of reading it—much faster than we understand its meaning. So when we read emotionally charged material, we reflexively react with feelings—fear, joy, awe, disgust, and so forth—because our brains have been trained since hunter-gatherer times to respond that way. Reason follows. We then combine the immediate feeling and subsequent thought to create meaning.

How sensitive are we to emotion? Experiments show that when people hear a list of words, they often miss a few as a result of "attentional blinks" caused by limits in our brain processing power. But we don't miss the emotionally significant words. With those there are no blinks.

So when you write your next memo, consider injecting words that package feeling and thought together. Instead of saying "challenge the competition," you might use "outwit rivals." In lieu of "promote innovation," try "prize ingenuity." Metaphor often works even better. Canadian researchers Andrea Bowes and Albert Katz tested relatively bland phrases like "What a very good idea!" and "Be careful what you say" against more-evocative expressions like "What a gem of an idea!" and "Watch your back." Readers reacted more strongly to the latter.

Just a small touch can drive the neural circuits for emotion. So before you start composing, get your feelings straight, along with your facts. Zeal for your message will show through. And if you express your emotion, readers will feel it.

Seductiveness

As humans, we're wired to savor anticipation. One famous study showed that people are often happier planning a vacation than they are after taking one. Scientists call the reward "anticipatory utility." You can build up the same sort of excitement when you structure your writing. In experiments using poetry, researchers found that readers' reward circuitry reached peak firing several seconds before the high points of emphatic lines and stanzas. Brain images show preemptive spikes of pleasure even in readers with no previous interest in poetry.

You can generate a similar reaction by winding up people's curiosity for what's to come. Steve Jobs did this in his famous "How to Live Before You Die" commencement address to Stanford University's class of 2005. "I never graduated from college," he began. "Truth be told, this is the closest I've ever gotten to a college graduation. Today I want to tell you three stories from my life. That's it. No big deal. Just three stories." Are you on the edge of your seat to hear what the three stories are?

So start a report with a question. Pose your customer problem as a conundrum. Position your product development work as solving a mystery. Put readers in a state of uncertainty so that you can then lead them to something better.

Smart Thinking

Making people feel smart—giving them an "aha" moment—is another way to please readers. To show how these sudden "pops" of insight activate the brain, researchers have asked people to read three words (for example, "house," "bark," and "apple") and then identify a fourth word that relates to all three, while MRI machines and EEGs record their brain activity. When the study participants arrive at a solution ("tree"), brain regions near the right temple light up, and so do parts of the reward circuit in the prefrontal cortex and midbrain. The readers' delight is visible. Psychological research also reveals how people feel after such moments: at ease, certain, and—most of all—happy.

How can you write to create an aha moment for your readers? One way is to draw fresh distinctions. Ginni Rometty, formerly IBM's CEO, offered one with this description of the future: "It will not be a world of man versus machine; it will be a world of man plus machine."

Another strategy is to phrase a pragmatic message so that it also evokes a perennial, universal truth. The late Max De Pree, founder and CEO of the office furniture company Herman Miller, had a knack for speaking to employees this way. In *Leadership Is an Art* he wrote: "The first responsibility of a leader is to define reality. The last is to say thank you. In between the two, the leader must become a servant and a debtor." That's wisdom not just for business managers but for parents, teachers, coaches—anyone in a guiding role.

Social Content

Our brains are wired to crave human connection—even in what we read. Consider a study of readers' responses to different kinds of literary excerpts: some with vivid descriptions of people or their thoughts, and others without such a focus. The passages that included people activated the areas of participants' brains that interpret social signals, which in turn triggered their reward circuits.

We don't want just to read about people, though—we want to understand what they're thinking as quickly as possible. A study led by Frank Van Overwalle, a social neuroscientist at Vrije Universiteit Brussel, found that readers infer the goals of people they're reading about in under 350 milliseconds, and discern their character traits within 650 milliseconds.

One way to help readers connect with you and your writing is to reveal more traces of yourself in it. Think voice, worldview, vocabulary, wit, syntax, poetic rhythm, sensibilities. Take the folksy—and effective—speeches and letters of Berkshire Hathaway CEO Warren Buffett. His bon mots include "Someone's sitting in the shade today because someone planted a tree a long time ago," "It's only when the tide goes out that you discover who's been swimming naked," and "Beware of geeks bearing formulas."

Remember also to include the human angle in any topic you're discussing. When you want to make a point about a supply-chain hiccup, for example, don't frame the problem as a "trucking disconnect." Write instead about mixed signals between the driver and dispatcher.

Another simple trick to engage readers is to use the second person ("you"), as I've done throughout this piece. This can be particularly helpful when you're explaining technical or complicated material. For example, psychologist Richard Mayer and colleagues at the University of California, Santa Barbara, ran experiments with two versions of an online presentation on the respiratory system. Each included 100 words of spoken text paired with simple animations. But one version used the impersonal third person ("During inhaling, *the* diaphragm moves down, creating more space for *the* lungs . . ."), while the other was more personal ("*your* diaphragm" and "*your* lungs"). People who listened to the latter scored significantly higher than their counterparts on a test that measured what they had learned.

Storytelling

Few things beat a good anecdote. Stories, even fragments of them, captivate extensive portions of readers' brains in part because they combine many of the elements I've described already.

Research by Uri Hasson at Princeton reveals the neural effect of an engaging tale. Functional MRI scans show that when a story begins, listeners' brains immediately begin glowing in a specific pattern. What's more, that grid reflects the storyteller's exactly. Other research shows that, at the same time, midbrain regions of the reward circuit come to life.

Experiments by behavioral scientists at the University of Florida produced similar results. Brain images showed heightened activity in reward regions among people who read 12-second narratives that prompted pleasant images. (A sample narrative: "It's the last few minutes of the big game and it's close. The crowd explodes in a deafening roar. You jump up, cheering. Your team has come from behind to win.")

When you incorporate stories into your communications, big payoffs can result. Consider research that Melissa Lynne Murphy did at the University of Texas, looking at business crowdfunding campaigns. She found that study participants formed more-favorable impressions of the pitches that had richer narratives, giving them higher marks for entrepreneur credibility and business legitimacy. Study participants also expressed more willingness to invest in the projects and share information about them. The implication: No stories, no great funding success.

The eight S's can be your secret weapons in writing well. They're effective tools for engaging readers because they trigger the same neural responses that other pleasurable stimuli do. And you probably understand their value intuitively because millions of years of evolution have trained our brains to know what feels right. So cultivate those instincts. They'll lead you to the writer's version of the Golden Rule: Reward readers as you would yourself.

Originally published in July–August 2021. Reprint R2104L

You Don't Just Need One Leadership Voice—You Need Many

by Amy Jen Su

WE OFTEN EQUATE DEVELOPING a leadership voice with finding ways to appear more confident. We assume that our success depends upon mimicking someone else, increasing our self-promotion, or saying things louder than others. But rather than living with imposter syndrome, or feeling exhausted by wearing your game face all day, you can build a truer confidence by focusing more intentionally on cultivating many different parts of your leadership voice each day. Ultimately, you should cultivate enough parts of your voice so that no matter the leadership situation or audience you face, you can respond in an authentic, constructive, and effective way. So, what are the various voices to access within yourself and cultivate over time? And what are the situations that warrant each voice?

Your voice of character.

First and foremost, consider the voice of your character. This is the part of your voice that is constant and consistent. It is grounded in fundamental principles about whom you choose to be and what guides and motivates your interactions with others. I've had leaders share that they hold key leadership principles in mind such as "Give the benefit of the doubt," "Don't take things personally," "Focus on what's best for the business," or "Be direct with respect" when walking into a difficult conversation, meeting, or potential conflict. Anchoring ourselves in the character we know we have keeps us from becoming chameleons, acting out of a fight-or-flight reaction, or only showing respect when there is a commercial gain or benefit—while being uncivil to others who we believe hold less value. A voice of character is ultimately about who you are and the intentions and motivations that guide your speech and actions.

Your voice of context.
As you take on increasingly senior roles, your view and perspective of the business grow. You hold more of the big picture. Part of the job then becomes finding ways to express and communicate that bigger picture to others. Too often, in the race against time, we dive right into the details of a presentation, meeting, or conversation, without taking a few extra minutes to appropriately set the stage and share critical context. Places where you can bring more of your voice of context include:

- Sharing vision, strategy, or upcoming organizational change with others

- Presenting to executives, and being clear on what you are there for and what you need

- Kicking off a meeting with your team and giving the bigger picture for the topic at hand

- Making your decision-making criteria or rationale transparent to others

Your voice of clarity.
In a world of high-intensity workplaces, you have the opportunity to be the voice of clarity and help your team stay focused on the most important priorities. Leaders who envision new possibilities, muse

Idea in Brief

The Goal

Many aspiring leaders focus on developing a more confident-sounding persona. But building true confidence starts with cultivating a multifaceted leadership voice, with enough parts that no matter the leadership situation or audience you face, you can respond in an authentic, constructive, and effective way.

The Path Forward

First, consider the voice of your character. This is the part of your voice that is grounded in fundamental principles about whom you choose to be and what guides

and motivates your interactions with others. Next, explore your voice of context: Instead of diving right into execution, take a moment to consider the strategic context of new initiatives. Third, leaders should aspire to be the voice of clarity, helping their team stay focused on the most important priorities. Fourth, cultivate your voice of curiosity, making sure that you're not approaching every situation as if you have all the answers. Finally, develop your voice of connection by improving your storytelling, expressing gratitude, and making time for your people.

out loud, or have knee-jerk reactions run the risk of teams trying to deliver on their every whim; these teams end up scattered, spread thin, and unfocused, falling short on delivering on the most important wins. Here are a few ways you can be the voice of clarity to help channel others' energies more productively:

- At the start of the year, sit down with each direct report to prioritize and clarify what the big wins are in each of their areas. One client of mine shared how she asks each team member: "If we were to publish this in a newspaper, what would you want the big headlines to be for you and your team at the end of the year?"

- Periodically come back to helping your direct reports reprioritize what's on their plates. You can do this in one-on-one meetings or with your entire team.

- Empower your team to say no.

Your voice of curiosity.
As a leader, you have a responsibility to give direction, share information, and make important decisions. But you need to be sure that you're not approaching every situation as if you have all the answers or as if you need to advise on, problem-solve, or fix everything in front of you. In many cases, being the voice of curiosity is a better choice for the situation. As one of my clients once shared about facing pushback from others, "While I'm confident in my own business judgment and instincts, I know that my organization has hired really smart people. Therefore, if one of my peers or team members has a different perspective or pushes back, I don't take it personally. I get really curious to understand where they are coming from first so that we can get to the best solution." Some situations where bringing your voice of curiosity can help you and your colleagues move forward:

- When you're engaging in work that is interdependent, and a better solution will come from hearing all perspectives in the room before coming to a final decision

- When you're coaching a direct report, and asking good questions will help them grow in new ways, explore issues they're facing, or support their career development

- When you're in a difficult conversation, where hearing out the other person is an important part of diffusing emotion, understanding each party's needs and views, and then figuring out the best way forward

Your voice of connection.
As your span of control or influence grows, it can become increasingly more difficult to make a connection with a broadening set of colleagues, strategic networks, and teams. We often have folks working for us many layers deep into the organization, such that we no longer know everyone in our area yet still must find ways to stay connected and visible. Being a voice of connection can come in many forms. Some of the ways I've seen others do this effectively:

- Increase your skill as a storyteller. Stories make our points more memorable and salient. They can enliven a keynote address or an all-hands meeting, drive home a point we're making in a presentation, or help to close a large deal or transaction.

- Thank and acknowledge. Our teams and colleagues often go to great lengths to ensure that deliverables are met, revenues are strong, and customers are satisfied. When we use our voice of connection, we remember to express gratitude to a team that worked through the holidays to close on the financials at the end of the quarter, or we remember to loop back with a colleague who made a valuable introduction or referral for us.

- Make time for a few minutes of ice-breaking or rapport-building at the start of a conversation or meeting. So often, we want to get right down to business, so we skip the niceties or pleasantries that help to build relationships with others. When possible, and especially with colleagues who value that kind of connection, take a couple of minutes to connect before getting down to work. On days when you're crunched for time, state it up front and transparently, so as not to create any misunderstandings. You can say something like: "I'm a little crunched for time today, so it would be great if we could dive right in."

Discovering and developing your voice as a leader is the work of a lifetime. The key is to stay open to an increasingly wide array of new situations and people. Use each situation as an opportunity to access more parts of your voice, rather than having a one-size-fits-all approach. Bring your voices of character, context, clarity, curiosity, and connection as the moment or situation warrants. Through this kind of learning and growth, not only will you increase your inner confidence and resilience, but you will also inspire the confidence of others around you in a more authentic and impactful way.

Reprinted from hbr.org, originally published January 10, 2018. Reprint HO43HT

Building an Ethical Career

by Maryam Kouchaki and Isaac H. Smith

MOST OF US THINK of ourselves as good people. We set out to be ethical, and we hope that in pivotal moments we will rise to the occasion. But when it comes to building an ethical career, good intentions are insufficient. Decades' worth of research has identified social and psychological processes and biases that cloud people's moral judgment, leading them to violate their own values and often to create contorted, post hoc justifications for their behavior. So how can you ensure that from day to day and decade to decade you will do the right thing in your professional life?

The first step requires shifting to a mindset we term *moral humility*—the recognition that we all have the capacity to transgress if we're not vigilant. Moral humility pushes people to admit that temptations, rationalizations, and situations can lead even the best of us to misbehave, and it encourages them to think of ethics as not only avoiding the bad but also pursuing the good. It helps them see this sort of character development as a lifelong pursuit. We've been conducting research on morality and ethics in the workplace for more than a decade, and on the basis of our own and others' findings, we suggest that people who want to develop ethical careers should consider a three-stage approach: (1) Prepare in advance for moral challenges; (2) make good decisions in the moment; and (3) reflect on and learn from moral successes and failures.

Planning to Be Good

Preparing for ethical challenges is important, because people are often well aware of what they *should* do when thinking about the future but tend to focus on what they *want* to do in the present. This tendency to overestimate the virtuousness of our future selves is part of what Ann Tenbrunsel of Notre Dame and colleagues call *the ethical mirage*.

Counteracting this bias begins with understanding your personal strengths and weaknesses. What are your values? When are you most likely to violate them? In his book *The Road to Character*, David Brooks distinguishes between *résumé* virtues (skills, abilities, and accomplishments that you can put on your résumé, such as "increased ROI by 10% on a multimillion-dollar project") and *eulogy* virtues (things people praise you for after you've died, such as being a loyal friend, kind, and a hard worker). Although the two categories may overlap, résumé virtues often relate to what you've done for yourself, whereas eulogy virtues relate to the person you are and what you've done for others—that is, your character.

So ask yourself: What eulogy virtues am I trying to develop? Or, as the management guru Peter Drucker asked, "What do you want to be remembered for?" and "What do you want to contribute?" Framing your professional life as a quest for contribution rather than achievement can fundamentally change the way you approach your career. And it's helpful to consider those questions early, before you develop mindsets, habits, and routines that are resistant to change.

Goal setting can also lay the groundwork for ethical behavior. Professionals regularly set targets for many aspects of their work and personal lives, yet few think to approach ethics in this way. Benjamin Franklin famously wrote in his autobiography about trying to master 13 traits he identified as essential for a virtuous life (including industry, justice, and humility). He even created a chart to track his daily progress. We don't suggest that everyone engage in

Idea in Brief

The Problem

Most of us think of ourselves as good people. We set out to be ethical at work, and we hope that in pivotal moments we will rise to the occasion. But when it comes to building an ethical career, good intentions are insufficient. Decades' worth of research has identified psychological processes and biases that cloud people's moral judgment, leading them to violate their own values, and often to create contorted, post hoc justifications for their behavior.

The Solution

How can we ensure that we will consistently do the right thing in our professional lives? It is necessary to shift mindset to *moral humility*—the recognition that we all have the capacity for ethical transgressions if we aren't vigilant. There is an effective three-stage approach for staying on the straight and narrow: Prepare in advance for moral challenges, including instituting proper safeguards; make good decisions in the moment; and reflect on and learn from moral successes and failures.

similarly rigid documentation, but we do suggest that you sit down and write out eulogy-virtue goals that are challenging but attainable. That is similar to what Clayton Christensen of Harvard Business School advocated in his HBR article "How Will You Measure Your Life?" After battling cancer, Christensen decided that the metric that mattered most to him was "the individual people whose lives I've touched."

Even the most carefully constructed goals, however, are still just good intentions. They must be fortified by personal safeguards—that is, habits and tendencies that have been shown to bring out people's better angels. For instance, studies suggest that quality sleep, personal prayer (for the religious), and mindfulness can help people manage and strengthen their self-control and resist temptation at work.

We also recommend "if-then planning"—what the psychologist Peter Gollwitzer calls *implementation intentions*. Dozens of research studies have shown that this practice ("If X happens, then I will do Y") can be effective in changing people's behavior, especially when such plans are voiced aloud. They can be simple but must also be specific, tying a situational cue (a trigger) to a desired behavior.

For example: *If* my boss asks me to do something potentially unethical, *then* I will turn to a friend or a mentor outside the organization for advice before acting. *If* I am solicited for a bribe, *then* I will consult my company's legal team and formal policies for guidance. *If* I witness sexual harassment or racial prejudice, *then* I will immediately stand up for the victim. Making if-then plans tailored to your strengths, weaknesses, values, and circumstances can help protect you against lapses in self-control, or inaction when action is required. But be sure to make your if-then plans *before* you encounter the situation—preparation is key.

Mentors, too, can help you avoid ethical missteps. When expanding your professional network and developing relationships with advisers, don't look only for those who can hasten your climb up the career ladder; also consider who might be able to support you when it comes to moral decisions. Build connections with people inside and outside your organization whose values are similar to yours and whom you can ask for ethics-related advice. Both of us have reached out to mentors for advice on ethical issues, and we teach our MBA students to do the same. Having a supportive network—and particularly a trusted ethical mentor—may also bring you opportunities to make a positive impact in your career.

Once you've made a commitment to living an ethical life, don't be shy about letting people know it. No one likes a holier-than-thou attitude, but subtle moral signaling can be helpful, particularly when it's directed at colleagues. You can do this by openly discussing potential moral challenges and how you would want to react or by building a reputation for doing things the right way. For example, in a study one of us (Maryam) conducted, participants were much less likely to ask an online partner to engage in unethical behavior after receiving an email from that partner with a virtuous quotation in the signature line (such as "Success without honor is worse than fraud").

Direct conversation can be tricky, given that people are often hesitant to discuss ethically charged issues. But if you think it's possible, we recommend engaging your coworkers, because ambiguity is a breeding ground for self-interested rationalization. Tactfully ask clarifying questions and make your own expectations clear: for example, "I think it's important that we don't cross any ethical lines here."

We are all shaped more by our environment than we realize, so it's also critical to choose a workplace that will allow if not encourage you to behave ethically. Not surprisingly, employees who feel that their needs, abilities, and values fit well with their organization tend to be more satisfied and motivated than their misaligned peers, and they perform better. Of course, many factors go into choosing a job— but in general people tend to overemphasize traditional metrics such as compensation and promotion opportunities and underemphasize the importance of the right *moral* fit. Our work and that of others has shown that ethical stress is a strong predictor of employee fatigue, decreased job satisfaction, lower motivation, and increased turnover.

Some industries seem to have cultural norms that are more or less amenable to dishonesty. In one study, when employees of a large international bank were reminded of their professional identity, they tended to cheat more, on average, than non-banker counterparts given the same reminder. This is not to say, of course, that all bankers are unethical, or that only unethical people should pursue careers in banking (although it does highlight how important it is for banks to prioritize hiring morally upstanding employees). We do suggest, however, that anyone starting a new job should learn about the organization and the relevant industry so as to prepare for morally compromising situations. Job interviews often conclude with the candidate's being asked, "Do you have any questions for me?" A possible response is "What types of ethical dilemmas might be faced in this job?" or "What does this company do to promote ethical business practices?"

Research also shows that elements of a work environment can enhance or diminish self-control, regardless of cultural norms: High uncertainty, excessive cognitive demands, long days and late nights, and consecutive stretch goals all correlate with increased rates of unethical behavior. Such pressures may wax and wane over time in your workplace, but during periods of intensity you should be extra vigilant.

Making Good Decisions

Even if you've planned for an ethical career and established safe-guards, it can be difficult to face moral challenges in the moment. Sometimes people overlook the implications of their decisions—or they find fanciful ways of rationalizing immoral, self-interested behavior. In other instances, they face quandaries in which the right decision isn't obvious—for example, a choice between loyalty to one's coworkers and loyalty to a customer, or a proposed solution that will produce both positive and negative externalities, such as good jobs but also environmental damage. There are several ways to manage moments of truth like these.

First, step back from traditional calculations such as cost-benefit analysis and ROI. Develop a habit of searching for the moral issues and ethical implications at stake in a given decision and analyze them using multiple philosophical perspectives. For instance, from the rule-based perspective of deontology (the study of moral obliga-tion), ask yourself what rules or principles are relevant. Will a certain course of action lead you to violate the principle of being honest or of respecting others? From the consequence-based perspective of utilitarianism, identify potential outcomes for all parties involved or affected either directly or indirectly. What is the greatest good for the greatest number of people? And from the Aristotelian perspec-tive of virtue ethics, ask yourself, Which course of action would best reflect a virtuous person? Each of these philosophies has advantages and disadvantages, but addressing the fundamental decision criteria of all three—rules, consequences, and virtues—will make you less likely to overlook important ethical considerations.

Note, however, that the human mind is skilled at justifying mor-ally questionable behavior when enticed by its benefits. We often tell ourselves things such as "Everyone does this," "I'm just follow-ing my boss's orders," "It's for the greater good," "It's not like I'm robbing a bank," and "It's their own fault—they deserve it." Three tests can help you avoid self-deceptive rationalizations.

1. *The publicity test.* Would you be comfortable having this choice, and your reasoning behind it, published on the front page of the local newspaper?

2. *The generalizability test.* Would you be comfortable having your decision serve as a precedent for all people facing a similar situation?

3. *The mirror test.* Would you like the person you saw in the mirror after making this decision—is that the person you truly want to be?

If the answer to any of these questions is no, think carefully before proceeding.

Studies also show that people are more likely to act unethically if they feel rushed. Very few decisions must be made in the moment. Taking some time for contemplation can help put things in perspective. In a classic social psychology experiment, students at Princeton Theological Seminary were much less likely to stop and help a stranger lying helpless on the ground if they were rushing to get to a lecture they were scheduled to give—on, ironically, the biblical parable of the Good Samaritan, which is about stopping to help a stranger lying helpless on the ground. So be aware of time pressures. Minding the old adage "Sleep on it" can often help you make better moral decisions. And delaying a decision may give you time to consult your ethical mentors. If they are unavailable, practice a variation on the mirror and publicity tests: Imagine explaining your actions to those advisers. If that would make you uncomfortable, be warned.

But taking an ethical stand often requires challenging coworkers or even superiors, which can be excruciatingly difficult. The now infamous Milgram experiments (wherein study participants administered potentially lethal shocks to innocent volunteers when they were instructed to do so by an experimenter) demonstrated how susceptible people can be to pressure from others—especially those in positions of power. How can you avoid succumbing to social pressure? The authors of *The Business Ethics Field Guide* offer a few questions to ask yourself in such situations: Do they have a right to request that I do this? Would others in the organization feel the same way I do about this? What are the requesters trying to accomplish? Could it be accomplished in a different way? Can I refuse to comply in a manner that helps them save face? In general, be wary of doing anything just because "everybody else is doing it" or your boss told you to. Take ownership of your actions.

And don't forget that many ethical challenges people face at work have previously been confronted by others. As a result, companies often develop specific guidelines, protocols, and value statements. If in doubt about a certain situation, try consulting the formal policies of your organization. Does it have an established code of ethics? If not, ask your ethical mentor for guidance. And if you're dealing with something you view as clearly unethical but fear reprisal from a superior, check to see whether your organization has an ombudsman program or a whistle-blowing hotline.

Reflecting After the Fact

Learning from experience is an iterative, lifelong pursuit: A lot of growth happens after decisions are made and actions taken. Ethical people aren't perfect, but when they make mistakes, they review and reflect on them so that they can do better in the future. Indeed, a wide array of research—in fields as diverse as psychology, computer science, nursing, and education—suggests that reflection is a critical first step in learning from past personal experiences. Reflecting on both successes and failures helps people avoid not only repeated transgressions but also "identity segmentation," wherein they compartmentalize their personal and professional lives and perhaps live by a very different moral code in each.

But self-reflection has limitations. Sometimes ethical lapses are obvious; other times the choice is ambiguous. What's more, people can be hemmed in by their own perspectives as well as by their personal histories and biases. That's why we should seek the counsel of people we trust. You can approach this as you would job performance feedback: by asking specific questions, avoiding defensiveness, and expressing gratitude.

Finally, you can engage in what Amy Wrzesniewski of Yale calls *job crafting:* shaping your work experiences by proactively adapting the tasks you undertake, your workplace relationships, and even how you perceive your job, such that work becomes more meaningful and helps you fulfill your potential. You can apply job crafting to your ethical career by making bottom-up changes to your work and the way you approach it that will help you be more virtuous. For example, in some of the earliest studies on job crafting, Wrzesniewski and colleagues found that many hospital housekeepers viewed their work in a way that made them feel like healers, not janitors. They didn't just clean rooms; they helped create a peaceful healing environment. One custodian used her smile and humor to help cancer patients relax and feel more comfortable. She looked for opportunities to interact with them, believing that she could be a momentary bright spot in the darkness of their ongoing chemotherapy. She crafted her job to help her develop and cultivate eulogy virtues such as love, compassion, kindness, and loyalty.

You may feel that it isn't all that difficult to be an ethical professional. As your parents may have told you, just do the right thing. But the evidence suggests that out in the real world it becomes increasingly difficult to remain on the moral high ground. So take control of your ethical career by cultivating moral humility, preparing for challenging situations, maintaining your calm in the moment, and reflecting on how well you've lived up to your values and aspirations.

Originally published in January–February 2020. Reprint R2001L

About the Contributors

ERIKA ANDERSEN is the founding partner of Proteus International. She is the host of *The Proteus Leader Show* podcast and the author of the books *Change from the Inside Out, Growing Great Employees, Being Strategic, Leading So People Will Follow,* and *Be Bad First.*

BILL BIRCHARD is a business writer and writing coach. His newest book is *Writing for Impact.* His previous books include *Merchants of Virtue, Stairway to Earth, Nature's Keepers,* and *Counting What Counts.* Learn more about the craft of writing at billbirchard.com.

RICHARD E. BOYATZIS is a professor in the departments of Organizational Behavior, Psychology, and Cognitive Science at the Weatherhead School of Management and Distinguished University Professor at Case Western Reserve University. He is a cofounder of the Coaching Research Lab and coauthor of *Helping People Change: Coaching with Compassion for Lifelong Learning and Growth* (Harvard Business Review Press, 2019).

ETHAN BURRIS holds the Neissa Endowed Professorship in Business and is the director of the Center for Leadership and Ethics at the McCombs School of Business at the University of Texas at Austin.

JOSEPH FULLER is a professor of management practice and a faculty cochair of the Project on Managing the Future of Work at Harvard Business School. He also cochairs Harvard's Project on Workforce, a collaboration among members of the faculty at the university's schools of business, education, and government.

AMY GALLO is a contributing editor at *Harvard Business Review,* cohost of the *Women at Work* podcast, and the author of two books: *Getting Along: How to Work with Anyone (Even Difficult People)* and the *HBR Guide to Dealing with Conflict.* She writes and speaks about workplace dynamics. Watch her TEDx talk on conflict and follow her on LinkedIn.

DANIEL GOLEMAN, best known for his writing on emotional intelligence, is codirector of the Consortium for Research on Emotional Intelligence in Organizations at Rutgers University. His latest book is *Building Blocks of Emotional Intelligence,* a 12-primer set on each of the emotional intelligence competencies, and he offers training on the competencies through an online learning platform, Emotional Intelligence Training Programs. His other books include *Primal Leadership: Unleashing the Power of Emotional Intelligence* and *Altered Traits.*

HEIDI GRANT is a social psychologist who researches, writes, and speaks about the science of motivation. Her most recent book is *Reinforcements: How to Get People to Help You.* She's also the author of *Nine Things Successful People Do Differently* and *No One Understands You and What to Do About It.*

STEPHEN HANSEN is an associate professor of economics at Imperial College Business School.

MANBIR KAUR is an executive coach and a conversational intelligence–enhanced skills practitioner. She is author of *Get Your Next Promotion* and *Are You the Leader You Want to Be?* (nominated for the C. K. Prahalad Business Book Award 2019).

MARYAM KOUCHAKI is a professor of management and organizations at the Kellogg School of Management. Her research explores ethics, morality, and the complexity and challenges of managing ethnic and gender diversity for organizations.

ERIN MEYER is a professor at INSEAD, where she directs the executive education program Leading Across Borders and Cultures. She is the author of *The Culture Map* and coauthor (with Reed Hastings) of *No Rules Rules.*

PJ NEAL is the global head of knowledge and operations for the Board & CEO Advisory Group at Russell Reynolds Associates.

RAFFAELLA SADUN is the Charles E. Wilson Professor of Business Administration at Harvard Business School.

ISAAC H. SMITH is an assistant professor of organizational behavior and human resources at BYU Marriott School of Business. His research explores the morality and ethics of organizations and the people in them.

MELVIN SMITH is a professor of organizational behavior at Case Western. He is a cofounder of the Coaching Research Lab and coauthor of *Helping People Change: Coaching with Compassion for Lifelong Learning and Growth* (Harvard Business Review Press, 2019).

AMY JEN SU is a cofounder and managing partner of Paravis Partners, a premier executive coaching and leadership development firm. For the past two decades, she has coached CEOs, executives, and rising stars in organizations. She is the author of *The Leader You Want to Be: Five Essential Principles for Bringing Out Your Best Self—Every Day* and coauthor of *Own the Room: Discover Your Signature Voice to Master Your Leadership Presence* with Muriel Maignan Wilkins.

ELLEN VAN OOSTEN is an associate professor of organizational behavior at Case Western. She is a cofounder of the Coaching Research Lab and coauthor of *Helping People Change: Coaching with Compassion for Lifelong Learning and Growth* (Harvard Business Review Press, 2019).

JAMIL ZAKI is a professor of psychology at Stanford University and author of *The War for Kindness*. His writing has appeared in the *New York Times*, the *Atlantic*, the *New Yorker*, and the *Wall Street Journal*.

Index

The most important management ideas all in one place.

We hope you enjoyed this book from *Harvard Business Review*. Now you can get even more with HBR's 10 Must Reads Boxed Set. From books on leadership and strategy to managing yourself and others, this 6-book collection delivers articles on the most essential business topics to help you succeed.

HBR's 10 Must Reads Series

The definitive collection of ideas and best practices on our most sought-after topics from the best minds in business.

- Change Management
- Collaboration
- Communication
- Emotional Intelligence
- Innovation
- Leadership
- Making Smart Decisions

- Managing Across Cultures
- Managing People
- Managing Yourself
- Strategic Marketing
- Strategy
- Teams
- The Essentials

hbr.org/mustreads

Engage with HBR content the way you want, on any device.

With HBR's subscription plans, you can access world-renowned case studies from Harvard Business School and receive four **free eBooks**. Download and customize prebuilt **slide decks and graphics** from our **Data & Visuals** collection. With HBR's archive, top 50 best-selling articles, and five new articles every day, HBR is more than just a magazine.

Subscribe Today
HBR.org/success